Praise for
Prince Andrew: Epstein and the Palace
by Nigel Cawthorne

'A strong book.'
WASHINGTON POST

'An irresistible story.'
NEWSWEEK

'Royal watcher tells all.'
NEW YORK POST

'Explosive exposé.'
GLOBE

'Controversial.'
OMID SCOBIE

'[A] psychological portrait.'
DAILY MAIL

'Excruciating details.'
SUNDAY TIMES

'Raises deep questions.'
A FINANCIAL TIMES BEST BOOK OF THE WEEK

'As forensic in detail… as salacious in delivery.'
TLS

A must-read.'
JEWISH CHRONICLE BOOK OF THE YEAR

'One of tl
many years.'

'What ı   g detail the
book goes into. An investigative look behind the key players, allegations, and counter-allegations… a different departure from the royal
family to the others in this round-up.'
THE I NEWSPAPER

'Goes behind the headlines, documentaries, and mini-series to
expose… the painstaking detail.'
INDEPENDENT

Also by Nigel Cawthorne

Prince Andrew: Epstein and the Palace
I Know I Am Rude but It Is Fun: Prince Philip on Prince Philip
Call Me Diana: The Princess of Wales in Her Own Words

This edition first published in the USA only by Gibson Square

rights@gibsonsquare.com
www.gibsonsquare.com
Tel: +1 646 216 9813 (USA)

ISBN   978-1-78334-217-4

CONTENTS

Ghislaine Maxwell, 38, Sotheby's vintage clothing sale 1999

Ghislaine Maxwell, 29, Moschino photoshoot 1990

INTRODUCTION

Multi-millionaire British socialite Ghislaine Maxwell seemed to live a charmed life. Based in New York, she was seen at all the best parties, not only in Manhattan but around the globe. Her friends included Presidents Donald Trump and Bill Clinton, along with just about everyone on the A-list worldwide. One of her oldest and closest friends was billionaire Jeffery Epstein, who had pleaded guilty to soliciting prostitution from a minor in Florida in 2008 under state law and received a light sentence. But to those in café society in Manhattan that did not really matter. There were other accusations against Epstein—some implicating Maxwell—but Epstein had more than enough money to keep his accusers at bay, for a time at least.

Unfortunately, Epstein and Maxwell had another friend—Prince Andrew, Duke of York, the second son of the Queen of England. In July 2019 Epstein was again arrested, but on far more serious federal sex trafficking charges involving the abuse of minors. He died mysteriously awaiting trial in jail a month later.

Andrew then made the mistake of going on British television in an attempt to draw a line under his association with Epstein.

1993, Ghislaine and Epstein first meet Bill Clinton as Epstein makes a donation to the refurbishment of the White House. She will later also befriend Chelsea Clinton.

This drew attention to a photograph that had first been published in 2011. It showed a young woman named Virginia Roberts, who later took the married name Giuffre. Standing next to her, with his arm around her waist, was Prince Andrew. In the background was Ghislaine Maxwell. According to Virginia Roberts Giuffre, the picture had been taken in Maxwell's London home and the man behind the camera was Epstein.

Giuffre's said that she had been recruited by Maxwell at the age of fifteen as a sex slave for

Epstein. She said that they had brought her over to London, age seventeen, to have sex with Prince Andrew—the first of three occasions. Maxwell denied this, saying she hardly knew the girl though she had settled a defamation case with her. Andrew said he had never met Miss Roberts and did not remember the photograph being taken, implying that it had been faked.ciation with Epstein.

Ghislaine and Epstein at a Mar-a-Lago party, 1995—federal charges brought against Ghislaine covered the years 1994-1997, 2001 and 2004

But Epstein was dead. Andrew was in England, beyond the jurisdiction of US courts, and was implicitly claiming some sort of royal privilege. Maxwell was at large in the US, so the young women who claimed that they had been victims of Epstein turned their fire on Maxwell, who they claimed had been his procurer. She went to ground.

Future President Donald Trump out on the town with Ghislaine, 1997

The FBI were not to be denied though. Once a grand jury had handed down an indictment, they tracked her down in July 2020. Previous charges against Maxwell had been settled out of court. This time, though, she faced federal charges. There was, as always, the possibility of a plea bargain.

Immediately there was speculation that she would throw Prince Andrew under the bus. Or Bill Clinton, or then President Donald Trump, who said: 'I wish her well'. Explaining his remark, he told Axios on HBO: 'Her boyfriend died in jail and people are still trying to figure out, how did it happen? Was it suicide? Was he killed? And I do wish her well. I'm not looking for anything bad for her.' Was that a veiled threat as Maxwell was being held in the same detention center where Epstein had died less than a year earlier?

Ghislaine and her university friend Prince Andrew, the Queen of England's favorite son, at the horse races at Royal Ascot, 2000

Or, if she persisted in pleading not guilty, would they be called as witnesses—either for the prosecution or the defense—ensuring that the hearings will be the trial of the century? Meanwhile Prince Andrew was staying schtum.

The deeper question remains: how was it that a woman born to wealth and privilege, who rubbed shoulders with royalty and was the toast of the champagne circuit, has been brought so low? Hubris or Nemesis?

I

TUCKEDAWAY

The residents of the sleepy town of Bradford, New Hampshire were woken at around 5am on July 2, 2020 by two small planes buzzing overhead. Puzzled residents began calling one another to try and find out what was going on. In a town with one set of traffic lights where nothing ever happens, something was afoot. A convoy was assembling. One local drove down to where some fifteen vehicles were lined up and demanded to know who they were and what they were doing. He was told they were from the New England Aerial Map Society.

Unfortunately, the local was an expert on geology and maps. It was what he did for a living and he knew that the New England Aerial Map Society did not exist. He asked to see inside their van, but was told it was off limits. Unwilling to be fobbed off, his wife called the police. But they were already there. The night before, the FBI had asked the local police and other agencies to join them on a dawn raid on a local mansion.

At 8.20am, the convoy set off into the New Hampshire woods. Heading a quarter of a mile up a steep dirt road, they passed a granite slab with name 'Tuckedaway' carved in it. They were then halted by brand new metal security gates. An FBI agent cut through the padlock. Then twenty-four agents stormed the $1-million home beyond. Two officers from the Internet Crimes Against Children task force were also on hand. Through a window, the agents saw a women wearing a T-shirt and jogging bottoms. She ignored their instructions to open the door and fled into an interior room, slamming a door behind her.

2020, The cathedral living room of 'Tuckedaway', Ghislaine Maxwell's hiding place in New Hampshire where she lived as 'Jen Marshall' with her husband

This was no courtesy call and the FBI did not

knock politely on the front door. Instead they used a battering ram to smash it down along with half the front wall, unhindered by the British ex-military personnel hired to guard the property. Bursting into the room where the fugitive had sought sanctuary, the FBI quickly handcuffed her. By 8.38am, she was in custody.

'Strangely, she didn't seem to have much reaction. It was like it wasn't registering with her,' said an arresting officer.

Although the woman in custody was not one of America's Most Wanted, she was notorious and had somehow eluded the authorities for nearly a year. This was British socialite Ghislaine Maxwell, the former girlfriend and confidante of billionaire pedophile Jeffery Epstein who died in jail on August 10, 2019. There were rumors that she was in a hideaway in Brazil, a safe house in Israel, or even in Russia where NSA whistleblower Edward Snowden had sought refuge. Closer to home she had been reported living in the quiet Massachusetts seaside town of Manchester-by-the-Sea in the mansion of former boyfriend Scott Borgerson, who denied any contact. Then a picture of her eating a burger and fries outside In-N-Out Burger in Los Angeles emerged, but the photograph had clearly been set up.

Dutch investigator Hank van Ess claimed on

Twitter that he had mapped Maxwell's movements across the US for fifty days from Doylestown, Pennsylvania, where she had visited a Dunkin' Donuts in the fall, to Bedford, New Hampshire, near where she was arrested. He described how he had first managed to identify her IP address by establishing that emails to her now defunct Terramar Project and messages sent to another of her email addresses were being opened by the same mobile phone. This allowed him to establish which cell tower she was near and plot her locations on a map.

During a search of her house, FBI agents found a cell phone wrapped in tin foil, perhaps in the mistaken belief that this would shield it from detection. On her bedside table they found a copy of the book *Relentless Pursuit: My Fight for the Victims of Jeffrey Epstein* by Bradley Edwards, a lawyer who represented fifty-six of Epstein's alleged victims.

'It's hard to tell exactly why she wanted to know what it was that I knew about her in the book,' the author said.

Others familiar with her predicament thought it was odd that she had remained in America. Maxwell had been born in France and had a French passport. France does not have an extradition treaty with the US. If she had fled there, the American authorities would not have been able to get her back. Indeed, in

June, the *Sun* reported she was spending lockdown in a flat in Paris' luxurious 8th Arrondissement owned by a wealthy France-based contact who knew she was laying low. As it was, she remained in the US, moving house as many thirty-six times during the year she was on the run.

'I would say she moved around three times a month. She took flights as well,' a friend said: 'Ghislaine has been constantly on the move throughout the last year. She would stay in properties for a few days or a week. Security guards were by her side due to death threats. She was never running from the Feds. She was running from journalists and crazy people who wanted to kill her. It was a serious problem. Her location was on a need-to-know basis.'

She visited Denver, Colorado, where the law firm representing her was based. She eventually settled in a hideaway in New Hampshire, along with a pet cat and two dogs, where she spent her days cooking and exercising and read a book written by British Prime Minister Boris Johnson—they were undergraduates at the same time at Balliol College, Oxford.

'She did go out, but not often,' the friend said. 'Obviously, with the Coronavirus, people were wearing masks—it made things easier for her.'

While Maxwell kept her head down, Lois Kilnapp, the boss of the town's recycling tip, said a long-haired

British man, aged around forty, had been coming from the mansion to dump since December. She knew he was from 338 East Washington Road— where Maxwell was later found—because she issued him with a $1 recycling permit for his pick-up truck.

'I became very friendly with him. He was a bit of a character and I like characters,' said Kilmapp. 'He was always smiling. I used to joke with him that he was the 'Duke of Sussex' because he led me to believe that he owned the home.'

In March, he told her he was heading back to the UK. He then introduced a second Brit to her, a man aged around fifty, who took over recycling duties.

'This guy wasn't as outgoing. He didn't really like to talk,' Kilmap said. 'Both men were big, rugged guys. I would guess that they were ex-military.'

When Maxwell was arrested, a British man named Martin was found living in a guesthouse in the grounds. He was a security guard from a UK firm. Described as a 'former Special Forces soldier,' he had been working there since at least March. The guard told the FBI that the defendant had not left the property during his time working there and he had been sent to make purchases for the property using a credit card.

The security firm was thought to have sent three or four British ex-servicemen to the property on rotation. The *Sun on Sunday* claimed Maxwell paid British veterans' firm The Next Step nearly $250,000. Run by an ex-SAS commando, it provided advice on 'preservation of life' and how to 'relocate,' but denied sending security to protect her.

2001, The infamous picture upstairs in Ghislaine's London house. Prince Andrew on the left, Ghislaine on the right and Virginia Giuffre in the middle. She recalled Epstein taking the picture on her visit to London.

Special Agent William Sweeney, assistant director in charge of the FBI's New York office, said: 'We have been discreetly keeping tabs on Maxwell's whereabouts as we worked this investigation and more recently we learned she had slithered away to a gorgeous property in New Hampshire, continuing to live a life of privilege while her victims lived with the trauma inflicted upon them years ago. We moved when we were ready.'

A source familiar with the hunt for Maxwell said: 'This has taken millions of dollars and hundreds of man hours. At least five million bucks, maybe more. The FBI has been tracking her for a year. They had her, then they lost her. She was in Colorado and Wyoming then they lost her until she showed up in New Hampshire. It's been a high-stakes game of cat and mouse.

'They had to build a case and put it in front of a grand jury. These things take time. She slipped through the net once but as soon as the grand jury came back with an indictment ten days ago, it was on.'

The federal charges on the indictment included one count of enticing a minor to travel to engage in illegal sex acts, one count of transporting a minor with the intent to engage in criminal sexual activity, and two counts of conspiracy concerning three victims—one of whom was thought to be Annie Farmer who claimed she was assaulted by Maxwell and Epstein at the age of sixteen. These offenses had taken place from at least 1994, when Maxwell had just moved to live in New York, through at least 1997. Then there were two counts of perjury made in sworn depositions in 2016 concerning a defamation case brought against her by Virginia Roberts Giuffre, the seventeen-year-old girl pictured with Ghislaine and Prince Andrew in Maxwell's townhouse in London, England. The defamation case was settled out of court, but the depositions Maxwell had made now roared back to life as criminal charges.

Maxwell had relatively recently moved to the luxury four-bedroom, mountain-top property set in 156-acres of woodland. She paid $1 million cash through a limited company in December to hide her identity. The broker who made the sale claimed that a British man attended the viewing and had put the company name Granite Reality LLC on the purchasing paperwork. The company was registered to an address in Boston shared by several companies including a law firm which had previously acted on behalf of Ms Maxwell.

'They said they didn't want her name known, so I thought it must be a movie star,' said the broker. 'She wanted to know what the flight patterns were over the house, which was very strange.'

The property had formerly been occupied by hikers and ramblers, and other people who wanted to spend time in the great outdoors. Hidden way, it was the perfect bolt hole. The realtors described the fantastic views from every room to Mt Sunapee foothills to the west.

Their website said: 'From the covered front porch to ceiling fieldstone fireplace, cathedral ceiling, and a spectacular chandelier, a wall of glass frames a stunning southwestern view beyond the stone patio.' Sotheby's called it 'an amazing retreat for the nature lover who also wants total privacy.'

According to US Attorney Alison Moe, Maxwell posed as a journalist named Jen Marshall to secretly purchase the sprawling New Hampshire hideaway where she was arrested.

'The real estate agent told the FBI agent the buyers for the house introduced themselves as Scott and Jen Marshall. Both had British accents,' said Moe. 'Scott Marshall told her he was retired from the British military and was currently working on a book. Jen Marshall described herself as a journalist. They told the agent they wanted to purchase the property quickly through a wire and they were setting up an LLC.'

The realtor realized Jen Marshall's true identity after seeing a picture of Maxwell.

Federal prosecutors said Maxwell had changed her phone number and email address, and had deliveries addressed to another name.

Dick Morris, a carpenter who lived nearby, said: 'I heard what I first thought was a para plane, basically an engine with a seat and parachute, which is common around here. You hear one for ten minutes and it's gone. But this went on and on.

'I went out to load my truck at 7am and the plane was still going. I thought, 'What the heck is this guy doing buzzing around and around?' I peered up through the trees and caught a glimpse of a small Cessna-type plane high up and buzzing in a wide circle.

'Then I noticed another plane so there were two of them, like opposite sides of a circle, this high-altitude circle of planes buzzing around and around. Later I realized it had to be the FBI making sure she didn't leave before the raid team got there.'

Following the high-stakes drama of the arrest, enforcement officers went out of their way to behave correctly. When the door was broken down, the terrified cat took off into the woods around her home which were inhabited by bears and porcupines.

'There were security people and highly paid lawyers out there looking in the woods. No-one wanted any harm to come to this poor creature,' a source close to the investigation told the *Daily Mail*. 'The irony is, the front door was unlocked so there was no reason to smash it down with a battering ram and cause so much chaos and damage. It was overkill and the poor cat was an innocent victim.'

The search went on for four days before the cat was found. The animal has been treated kindly and seems not to have suffered too much during its ordeal.

The same could not be said for Ms Maxwell who had been wrenched from the world of wealth and privilege she had enjoyed all her life.

Merrimack County Jail.

Multi-millionaire Ghislaine Maxwell had been taken from the comfort of her mansion to Merrimack County Jail twenty miles away in Boscawen, New Hampshire. The reception there was bleak. An insider at the prison said: 'The general opinion of her at Merrimack was that she's a snooty rich b****. Nobody wanted anything to do with her.'

2

JAILBIRD

After four sleepless nights in the county jail, Maxwell was transported, handcuffed and shackled, to the Metropolitan Detention Center in Brooklyn, where she was given a humiliating strip search and cavity examination. Gone were her Prada dresses and her Louboutin shoes. Her orange polyester jumpsuit was made of paper clothing as she was considered a suicide risk and she was given prison-issue slippers. Otherwise, one pair of trainers were allowed a year. It was a far cry from the stylish outfits she was accustomed to.

At first she was held in isolation in an 8ft by 10ft cell, furnished with a flimsy mattress, a blanket and a pillow—but no sheet. No personal possessions were permitted, though she was allowed a radio or MP3 player. A towel and a government-approved hygiene kit were supplied. She was woken at 6am and had to make her own bed by 7.30. Inmates were locked down for twenty-three hours a day. Her one hour of recreation took place in a small caged area close to her cell.

Metropolitan Detention Center in Brooklyn, one of the toughest jails in New York City

The then US Attorney General William Barr personally called prosecutors in the Southern District of Manhattan to say no harm must come to her. To keep her safe, she was moved from cell to cell. Sometimes she had a cellmate, sometimes not.

Former prison governor Cameron Lindsay previously said that the risks for a high-profile inmate like Maxwell are real.

'To take someone out like that, that would be a badge of honor in the subculture of prisons,' he said.

One of the inmates, however, reported: 'She was in deep shock at first, but she is getting better each day. She is not a whiner or complainer.'

However her hair was unkempt and her nails

unmanicured. Her phone calls were limited to fifteen minutes each, with a maximum of three hundred minutes allowed per month, and she was banned from having any 'nude or sexually suggestive' photos, according to Federal Bureau of Prisons regulations.

The Brooklyn Metropolitan Detention Center was not the same detention center where Epstein was held. But it was no better. A dusty lockup adjacent to the waterfront and expressway in Sunset Park, it's a place so notorious that a magistrate judge once said she was reluctant to send women there because of the 'unconscionable' conditions. It has been the subject of numerous complaints and scrutiny that rivaled that of the rat-infested federal Metropolitan Correctional Center lockup in Lower Manhattan where Epstein lost his life. Former inmates include Donald Trump's lawyer and fixer Michael Cohen, firebrand minister Al Sharpton, British terrorist Abid Naseer, and R&B star R. Kelly, also there on charges of sex trafficking underage girls.

Over the years, federal investigators have concluded the Brooklyn jail was among the worst in the US Bureau of Prisons system. Prisoners have been beaten, raped, or held in inhumane conditions. In early 2019, hundreds of inmates at this detention center were locked shivering in their cells for at least a week after an electrical fire knocked out power in the building.

THE FALL OF AMERICA'S MOST NOTORIOUS SOCIALITE

The inmates spent some of the coldest days of the winter in darkness, without heating or hot water. Inmates die with regularity.

Cheryl Pollak, the federal magistrate in Brooklyn who visited the facility, found that 161 female inmates were held in two large rooms that lacked windows, fresh air or sunlight, twenty-four hours a day, seven days a week, and weren't allowed out to exercise.

'Some of these conditions wouldn't surprise me if we were dealing with a prison in Turkey or a Third World Country,' she said. 'It's hard for me to believe it's going on in a federal prison.'

Maxwell was lucky in one way though. The correctional facility was ill-equipped to deal with the Covid-19 pandemic cases. But as she was to be held in solitary confinement, the late fifty-something year old was more protected from infection than her fellow Brooklyn inmates. Otherwise, inmates were locked down with bunk beds barely six feet apart, unable to leave their bunks except to use the bathroom or shower. They weren't given gloves, hand sanitizer, or disinfectant wipes. Those suffering from symptoms couldn't be tested.

Clearly Maxwell was not used to such harsh conditions, even though she had been to a British boarding school which many offending alumni said prepared them for prison life.

In a desperate bid to get her out, her lawyers proposed that she be released on a $5 million bond under some conditions, including that she be placed under GPS monitoring. The bail application was signed by six of her associates, including two of her sisters, and secured by a $3.75 million property in Britain.

Maxwell's lawyers complained that she was being treated as a scapegoat. It was suggested by her lawyers that she could be put up in a luxury hotel rather than a jail while awaiting trial.

'On August 10, 2019, Epstein died in federal custody, and the media focus quickly shifted to our client – wrongly trying to substitute her for Epstein – even though she'd had no contact with Epstein for more than a decade, had never been charged with a crime or been found liable in any civil litigation, and has always denied any allegations of claimed misconduct.'

She insisted her romance with Epstein ended in 2001 and she had not seen him in person after 2005 when she was photographed with her at a party. However, court filings from the Giuffre defamation case 2015, unsealed on August 9, 2020, the day before Epstein's death, include a log of email communications between Maxwell and Epstein, showing they contacted each other between January 6 and January 27, 2015. This was around the time when Giuffre launched a defamation suit against Maxwell.

Details of the content of the emails could not be revealed as Harvard law professor Alan Dershowitz was included in one, so they were protected by attorney-client privilege. In a court filing against Epstein's estate in the Virgin Islands, Maxwell claimed she worked for Epstein or his companies until 2006. That year, she took fourteen flights on Epstein's private jet. She flew to Paris on Epstein's Boeing 727 on his fifty-fourth birthday in January 2007. Whether she flew on his jet afterwards couldn't be established as the following month Epstein's pilots stopped writing down the names of passengers with a 53-page indictment being filed against Epstein in June that year.

Prosecutors, however, strenuously argued that Maxwell should not be allowed bail as she 'poses an extreme risk of flight' with extensive international ties and citizenship of two foreign countries.

'In short, Maxwell has three passports, large sums of money, extensive international connections, and absolutely no reason to stay in the United States and face the possibility of a lengthy prison sentence,' prosecutors wrote. 'The incentive to flee is especially strong for this defendant who, at age fifty-eight, faces the very real prospect of spending a substantial portion of the rest of her life in prison.'

The prosecutors added: 'To the extent the defendant now refuses to account for her ownership of or access to vast wealth, it is not because it does not exist—it is because she is attempting to hide it… there should be no question that the defendant is skilled at living in hiding.'

Maxwell's cell phone, found in her New Hampshire home, all of a sudden took center stage.

Prosecutors said: 'Moreover, as the agents conducted a security sweep of the house, they also noticed a cell phone wrapped in tin foil on top of a desk, a seemingly misguided effort to evade detection, not by the press or public, which of course would have no ability to trace her phone or intercept her communications, but by law enforcement.'

They pressed home the point of her being at risk of fleeing from the US as she had 'absolutely no reason to stay. She has no children, does not reside with any immediate family members, and does not appear to have any employment that would require her to remain in the United States. Nor does she appear to have any permanent ties to any particular location in the United States.

'Because there is no set of conditions short of incarceration that can reasonably assure the defendant's appearance, the government urges the court to detain her.'

Maxwell's defense team said she would surrender

her US, British and French passports and would confine herself to a property in New York where she could be monitored electronically. They claimed that, for the last year, she had not been hiding from prosecutors, but from an 'unrelenting and intrusive media,' and that she too was a victim of Epstein's.

'The media attention spawned a carnival-like atmosphere of speculation about her whereabouts,' said her lawyers. She had seen helicopters flying over her home and reporters hiding in the bushes.

Curiously, Maxwell's lawyers refused to reveal the one fact that would show to the judge that she did have at least one reason to stay in the US. In 2016, she had married Bostonian Scott Borgerson, a tech multi-millionaire. In her pre-trial disclosures to the court, Maxwell admitted she was married, but refused to say to whom. It would be the British *Telegraph* newspaper that would reveal his name in December 2020. At that time, it would also become known that, although his estimated wealth was over $100 million, she had transferred her entire fortune of $28.5 million to him upon the marriage. Did she want the judge who decided whether she could be relied on sticking to bail conditions not to know about this strange marital arrangement?

Prosecutors argued that she couldn't be trusted as she had behaved suspiciously ever since the bombshell arrest of Jeffrey Epstein. She shouldn't be released on bond because she was hiding from law enforcement for over a year, making 'intentional efforts to avoid detection' like moving homes twice, registering a new phone number under a different name, and paying for her New Hampshire mansion with cash.

Scott Borgerson, Ghislaine's husband since 2016, whose name she didn't want to reveal when she was arrested.

In a memo filed on July 10, her lawyers desperately countered: 'She did not flee, but rather left the public eye, for the entirely understandable purpose of protecting herself and those close to her from the crush of media and online attention and its very real harms—those close to her have suffered the loss of jobs, work opportunities, and reputational damage simply for knowing her...'

'Ever since Epstein's arrest, Ms. Maxwell has been at the center of a crushing onslaught of press articles, television specials, and social media posts painting her in the most damning light possible and prejudging her guilt. The sheer volume of media reporting mentioning Ms Maxwell is staggering.'

They thought that, after Epstein's death, open season had been declared on Maxwell and her behavior was entirely reasonable.

'She has been the target of alarming physical threats, even death threats, and has had to hire security guards to ensure her safety. The media feeding frenzy, which has only intensified in recent months, has also deeply affected her family and friends,' they said.

Her legal team insisted that she 'has never once attempted to hide from the government or her accusers, and has never shown any intent to leave the country.' They claimed that rather than hide, she contacted federal prosecutors through her lawyers shortly after Epstein's arrest, and they had maintained regular contact with them. Maxwell would have also been willing to turn herself in if authorities had advised them of her impending arrest. Even so, ostensibly undermining Maxwell's willingness to be cooperative, they refused to disclose to the judge the simple fact who Maxwell was married to.

The memo also stated that Maxwell 'vigorously denies the charges, intends to fight them, and is entitled to the presumption of innocence,' and should be granted bail because of the Covid-19 threat in jail where fifty-five inmates and staff had tested positive for the virus through June 30.

The memo went on: 'As this court has noted, the Covid-19 pandemic represents an unprecedented health risk to incarcerated individuals, and Covid-19-related restrictions on attorney communications with pre-trial detainees significantly impair a defendant's ability to prepare her defense.... Simply put, under these circumstances, if Ms Maxwell continues to be detained, her health will be at serious risk and she will not be able to receive a fair trial.'

They underlined again: 'Ghislaine Maxwell is not Jeffrey Epstein.' Epstein victim Virginia Giuffre, however, countered publicly that Ghislaine was worse. Without Maxwell, Epstein would not have been able to operate. She herself had been recruited by Maxwell while she was working, age sixteen, as a spa attendant at Donald Trump's Mar-a-Lago Club in Florida while reading a book on massage therapy. 'This beautiful, well spoken, well-mannered woman with an English accent, prim and proper' approached her she told NBC news. She had suffered from sexual abuse as a child, but, she said, Maxwell's elegant manners and appearance raised no alarm bells whether the introduction to her rich friend Epstein was going to turn out to be unsavory.

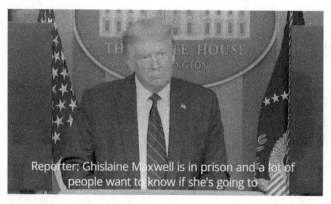

President Trump wishes Ghislaine well on 22 July and on 4 August 2020 saying that her 'boyfriend' Epstein may have been 'killed' despite a prison inquiry concluding it was suicide

The charges against Maxwell were serious. Federal prosecutors alleged in the six-count indictment against Maxwell that she took part 'in the sexual exploitation and abuse of multiple minor girls by Jeffrey Epstein.' From 1994 to at least 1997, 'Maxwell assisted, facilitated, and contributed to Jeffrey Epstein's abuse of minor girls by, among other things, helping Epstein to recruit, groom, and ultimately abuse victims known to Maxwell and Epstein to be under the age of eighteen.' Some of the alleged victims were as young as fourteen.

Maxwell's lawyers tried to argue that the charges against Maxwell were covered by a 2007 non-prosecution agreement that Epstein signed with federal prosecutors in Florida. Under this plea-bargain, Epstein agreed to plead guilty in Florida state court to two charges under Florida law for solicitation of prostitution, one of them with a minor, register as a sex offender, and pay restitution to three dozen victims identified by the FBI. In exchange, the federal prosecutor gave Epstein and his associates a real sweet-heart deal. Epstein was granted immunity from all federal criminal charges and all federal grand jury indictments were dropped. Immunity was extended as well to four named co-conspirators—thought to be Sarah Kellen, Adriana Ross, Lesley Groff, and Nadia Marcinkova— and any unnamed 'potential co-conspirators.' This would have included Maxwell they pleaded before the judge.

Her lawyers pointed out: 'She was not named in the government's indictment of Epstein in 2019, despite the fact that the government has been investigating this case for years. Instead, the current indictment is based on allegations of conduct that allegedly occurred roughly twenty-five years ago.'

Meanwhile one of Epstein's victims began civil proceedings for damages, claiming that Maxwell was Epstein's chief facilitator and believed she should bear responsibility for her actions. Others were expected to follow suit. A well-placed legal source said: 'We expect an avalanche of cases to come forward now.'

In a bombshell TV interview, then US Attorney General Barr made it clear that the Department of Justice would also like to interview Prince Andrew as part of their investigation. In June 2020, the DoJ made a formal request to the British government for his testimony in the Maxwell case under a Mutual Legal Assistance Treaty. If Prince Andrew visited the US, he could be arrested as the first British royal running that risk since the Declaration of Independence. In those circumstances, he would have to give evidence as a material witness in the case.

Newsweek reported that a majority of British subjects believe Andrew should be stripped of his titles and extradited to the United States. US public opinion concurred, but extradition would only be applicable if Prince Andrew faced criminal charges in the US. As it was Prince Andrew did not travel the US to give evidence to the FBI to shed light on the case against his friend Ghislaine Maxwell.

Attorney Gloria Allred, who represented sixteen of Epstein's alleged victims, suggested that Prince Andrew should talk to the Federal authorities in New York before Maxwell did.

'If I were Prince Andrew, I would want to speak to prosecutors before Ms. Maxwell speaks to the prosecutors. And the clock is ticking. She could decide to speak with them at any time,' she said. This advice fell on deaf ears at Buckingham Palace in Britain.

Meanwhile Maxwell sought to prevent the release of court documents that revealed the names of hundreds of people—some very high profile—allegedly linked to Epstein who may need to be notified before any disclosure.

Jeffrey Pagliuca, Maxwell's lawyer, said: 'There are probably hundreds of people that would need to be designated.'

The documents also include eighty-eight-pages of reports compiled by the police in Palm Beach, summaries of flight logs from Epstein's private jet dubbed the 'Lolita Express' and a 418-page deposition of her own words in testimony she provided for a defamation case with Virginia Giuffre. Pagliuca and his team said the sealed documents also included 'intrusive questions about her sex life.'

'The subject matter of these [documents] is extremely personal, confidential and subject to considerable abuse by the media,' her lawyers said. 'Courts must exercise their supervisory power over their own records and files to ensure they are not used to gratify private spite or promote public scandal.'

Fearing that Maxwell may also be planning to strike a sweetheart deal with prosecutors, Giuffre tweeted: 'Seriously America, wtf is going on?'

The prosecutors remained adamant. More witnesses had come forward who were willing to provide 'detailed, credible' evidence 'which has the potential to make the Government's case even stronger.'

'At the heart of this case are brave women who are victims of serious crimes that demand justice,' prosecutors said. 'The defendant's motion wholly fails to appreciate the driving force behind this case: The defendant's victims were sexually abused as minors as a direct result of Ghislaine Maxwell's actions, and they have carried the trauma from these events for their entire adult lives.'

The prosecutors argued that if the defendant was bailed, the victims would be denied justice.

On July 14, Maxwell appeared at a federal courthouse in Manhattan by video link to plead not guilty. US District Judge Alison Nathan scheduled Maxwell's trial to begin on July 12, 2021.

As part of the government's presentation, Assistant U.S. Attorney Alison Moe read aloud a statement by one victim, accusing her of 'calculating and sadistic manipulation.'

'Without Ghislaine, Jeffrey could not do what he did,' the woman said.

Annie Farmer, another of Epstein's victims, gave a very short statement by phone asking the court to detain Maxwell. Farmer said: 'I met Ghislaine Maxwell when I was sixteen years old. She is a sexual predator who groomed and abused me and countless other children and young women. She has never showed any remorse for her heinous crimes or the devastating, lasting affects her actions caused.'She said Maxwell 'lied under oath and tormented her survivors.' The indictment alleged that she helped groom the victims to endure sexual abuse and was sometimes there when Epstein abused them.

Annie Farmer in 1996, Ghisllaine said 'She is perfect' according to her sister Maria

Farmer said Maxwell 'has associates across the globe, some of great means and is a significant flight risk.'

'We may never know how many people were victimized by Ghislaine Maxwell but those of us who survived implore this court to detain her until she is forced to stand trial and answer for her crimes.'

Maria Farmer the year before she entered art school and met Ghislaine and Epstein

Annie Farmer's allegations were first made by her sister Maria, a painter, to the FBI and NYPD in Manhattan in 1996. Neither investigated further. Subsequently she also spoke in 2002 to a *Tatler* journalist who was doing a profile on Epstein, but the magazine did not include Farmer's testimony. Assistant US Attorney Moe said Maxwell had 'not come close' to disclosing her true financial assets to the court and emphasized 'serious red flags' in her character and wealth, making her an extreme flight risk if released. She said Maxwell's lawyer's contacts with the feds 'have not been substantial' and didn't include information on her whereabouts. As with the name of her husband, her lawyers declined to disclose in July 2020 what had happened to her almost $30 million fortune, even though prosecutors could trace transactions of tens of millions going through Maxwell's bank accounts.

Moe said Maxwell told the court's pretrial services department that she had fewer than $1 million in Swiss bank accounts and no income, but prosecutors feel that her current lifestyle makes that unlikely.

'It just doesn't make sense,' Moe told the court. 'Either there are other assets, or there is other income.'

Maxwell wasn't forthcoming with information. She told investigators she didn't know who bought the New England mansion, but a real estate agent identified her to the FBI as the woman who called herself Jen Marshall she met and accompanied on a tour of the home, a prosecutor said.

'She has the ability to live off the grid indefinitely,' Moe said.

Prosecutors said the British heiress failed to provide financial information, despite allegedly having access to more than $20 million across at least a dozen bank accounts since 2016. 'To the extent [Maxwell] now refuses to account for her ownership of or access to vast wealth, it is not because it does not exist—it is because she is attempting to hide it,' prosecutors wrote.

The prosecutors also said that victims' testimony was corroborated by other witnesses and documentary evidence including diary entries, flight records, and business records. They said they'd 'been in touch with additional individuals who have expressed a willingness to provide information' on Maxwell, and that 'has the potential to make the government's case even stronger.'

After hearing all the arguments from Moe and Maxwell's attorney Mark S. Cohen, Judge Nathan gave his ruling.

'Not only does the defendant have significant financial resources, but she has demonstrated sophistication in hiding those resources and herself,' Nathan said. 'The court finds by a preponderance of evidence that no combination of conditions could reasonably assure her presence at court.' Judge Nathan ordered her to be held without bail pending trial.

In a statement, Virginia Roberts Giuffre said she was 'thrilled.'

'Without Ghislaine, Jeffrey Epstein would not have been able to fulfill his sick desires,' Giuffre said. 'Ghislaine preyed on me when I was a child. As with every other of her and Jeffrey Epstein's victims, I will have to live with what she did to me for the rest of my life. The rest of her life should be spent behind bars.'

Certainly the next twelve months would be spent behind bars in conditions her former life of luxury and privilege could not have prepared her for.

3

POOR LITTLE RICH GIRL

Ghislaine Maxwell was born on Christmas Day 1961, in Maisons-Laffitte, an affluent suburb northwest of Paris, France. Her French mother, Elisabeth 'Betty' Meynard was the daughter of a prosperous Protestant silk weaver, an academic then studying to become a lawyer. She met Robert Maxwell, a Czech serving in the British Army, at the liberation of Paris in 1944. They met at the French Welcome Committee in the Place de la Madeleine, where Allied soldiers could socialize with French civilians. They married in Paris on March 14, 1945, before moving to England.

Betty was a Protestant; Robert Maxwell was Jewish. He had been born Ján Ludvík Hyman Binyamin Hoch in Slatinské Doly, Czechoslovakia, now Solotvyno in the Ukraine on the border with Romania. At the beginning of World War II, he escaped to France where he joined the Czechoslovak

Army in exile in May 1940. His parents, grandfather and three of his siblings who remained behind died in Auschwitz. After the fall of France, he fled to England where he joined the North Staffordshire regiment and, due to his talent for languages, was recruited into intelligence, adopting the surname 'Ivan du Maurier', taking his surname from his favorite brand of cigarette. He won the Military Cross for heroism and was promoted to captain. He changed his name yet again, to 'Robert Maxwell', after he naturalized as a British subject in 1946. This name stuck and he was known at Cap'n Bob for the rest of his life.

After the collapse of the Third Reich he had become a member of the branch of the Allied Control Commission in Berlin responsible for licensing films, plays, books, and newspapers. Rumors were that he also began a working relationship with the KGB at that time.

Maxwell used his time in Berlin well. He would make business contacts that led to the purchase of his first company, a publisher of scientific journals and textbooks that he bought from its German and British owners and renamed Pergamon Press. It was alleged that MI6 funded the company as a cover for spying on the Soviet bloc countries where Maxwell increasingly did his business, ingratiating himself by publishing fawning biographies of Communist dictators. He was also thought to have been connected to the Israeli secret service Mossad.

Despite of his impressive war and secret-service credentials, the *Oxford Dictionary of National Biography* sums him up merely as 'publisher and swindler'. One reason was that Maxwell tried in 1969 to sell Pergamon Press to New York financier Saul P. Steinberg, who pulled out of the deal when he discovered that Maxwell had improperly inflated the company's value. This became national news as in 1964 Maxwell had become a Labour Member of Parliament for Buckingham. He was ambitious and high profile, but failed in his ambition to become a government minister. Maxwell was ousted from the board and also lost his parliamentary seat in the 1970 general election.

A protracted British government investigation ensued under the Conservative government and it concluded that Maxwell was not 'a person who can be relied on to exercise proper stewardship of a publicly quoted company.' Nevertheless, by going heavily into debt, he succeeded in buying the company back—and earning the nickname the 'Bouncing Czech.'

While Robert Maxwell focused all his energies on this business career, Betty stayed at home, producing nine children, seven of whom survived childhood.

The children were brought up as Anglicans. Her role, Betty said, was to recreate the family her husband had lost in the war. She later returned to university and studied the Holocaust.

Baby Ghislaine (the youngest in the middle) with her parents and older siblings.

Ghislaine was the youngest of the children and thought to be her father's favorite. Two days after she was born her fifteen-year-old brother Michael, who Maxwell hoped would one day inherit his empire, suffered irreversible brain damage in a car accident when a Pergamon driver fell asleep at the wheel and collided with a truck. Michael never regained consciousness before dying seven years later. The loss traumatized the family, which had already lost a daughter Karine who died of leukemia in 1957, age three.

Ghislaine's father with heirs to the throne Prince Charles and Prince William.

In her father's eyes, Ghislaine became a preor-
dained replacement for Michael. Hers was the only
family photograph on display in his office. But while
she was the apple of her father's eye, her mother
Betty admitted that she woefully neglected her
youngest daughter while looking after her oldest son
Michael in hospital hoping against hope that he
would recover. She was devastated when the three-
year-old Ghislaine said simply: 'Mummy, I exist'.
Betty only marginally took more notice. Between
these two extreme parents, Ghislaine as a child

became depressed and anorexic as a toddler, her mother said.

The family lived on the outskirts of Oxford, England, at Headington Hill Hall, a lofty fifty-three-room Italianate mansion set in fourteen acres, mocked as 'Versailles on the hill.' Under previous ownership it had been visited by Oscar Wilde and members of the artistic Bloomsbury Group. Maxwell acquired it for the peppercorn rent of $3,500 a year from the city authorities in Oxford. Because his land-lord was the city, the magnate who was born in a hovel would often joke with considerable understate-ment that his sumptuous home was Britain's most luxurious housing project.

Headington Hill Hall, nr Oxford, where Ghislaine grew up.

In fact, its atmosphere was even more menacing.

Despite having its own swimming pool and tennis courts, the estate was surrounded by barbed wire and guards. You could not get in or out without Cap'n Bob's permission.

Maxwell held stars-studded parties there. He even commissioned a stained-glass window by an Israeli sculptor Nehemia Azaz to adorn the imperial staircase and the walls were bedecked with giant portraits of the man himself, like the Communist-bloc despots he purported to admire.

The temporary loss of Pergamon Press caused deep ructions in the family, not least because Headington Hall was also the headquarters of the company. At eight, Ghislaine was too young to understand what was happening. She started seeking attention by behaving badly at school and her grades slipped. Her headmistress decided that Ghislaine was not very bright and recommended that she be removed from school and see a psychotherapist.

Instead Betty took Ghislaine to a specialist in Oxford who conducted a series of tests on her, concluding that she was highly intelligent and was simply at the wrong type of school. She needed a complete change of environment and recommended that she be sent to boarding school.

They found a mixed prep school named Edgarley Hall in Somerset that had an excellent reputation.

Ghislaine was happy there and her behavior changed almost over night. Even her academic results improved in the end. At thirteen she returned to Oxford to attend the exclusive Headington Girls' School, where she was very sporty at tennis, hockey and athletics.

Her family's ostentatious wealth made Ghislaine the butt of teasing at school. She was also taunted for her slow reading and responded by bullying, a ploy taken from her father's playbook. Robert Maxwell would invite Ghislaine's classmates up to the hall to take part in reading competitions. No matter how good the other girls were, Ghislaine was declared the winner every time.

Domestically, as in business, Maxwell was a domineering, intensively possessive, and demanding parent who humiliated his children and made their home life almost unbearable. He demanded unconditional obedience from his dependents and relished shows of magnanimity after blistering rows. Ruling by fear, Maxwell hated to lose, loved to humiliate, and used psychological pressure of intimidation or love over everyone, especially his family.

During a marital crisis of 1980-81 his wife wrote a letter to him describing him as 'harsh, cruel, uncompromising, dictatorial, exceedingly selfish and inconsiderate, totally unaware of the feelings of others, least of all those who are loyal and devoted to you, those you take a sadistic pleasure in crushing and humiliating.'

Ghislaine, anorexic as a toddler, neglected by her mother, bullied by her father.

It made no difference. He would make up with his wife and things continued as before. Maxwell would question his children on world affairs. If they made a mistake, he would erupted with rage and physically beat the child in front of everyone, including any visitors. They were both terrified of him and loved him unconditionally. Even Ghislaine suffered her father's merciless bullying, especially over Sunday lunch where attendance was compulsory.

'He was never satisfied,' said his wife Betty, who he came to loathe over the last fifteen years of his life.

'Everything was sacrificed on the altar of Bob's genius and in the end the children and I were to pay a heavy price.'Robert Maxwell's biographer Tom Bower had known Ghislaine from the age of eleven. When Robert Maxwell had fallen on hard times, Bower said he watched her snuggle up to her father while he showed an unusual mixture of kindness and control to his youngest child.

She also took on some of his most loathsome qualities. 'He encouraged her to adopt his worst characteristics of arrogance and rudeness, tempered by charm when required,' said Bower. 'She also inherited her father's lust for wealth and power.'

In Bower's eyes, this explained much about her later life. Despite her father's maltreatment of her, Ghislaine idolized her father and sought out men like him.

'She worshipped rich, domineering men,' he said. The manipulative billionaire Jeffrey Epstein seemed to have been made for her.

In public, however, Maxwell was fiercely protective of his daughter, who he called 'Sprog,' and he could be remarkably generous to make her look good. A school friend recalled returning from Ghislaine's opulent birthday parties at Headington Hill Hall laden with extravagant goodies including, on one occasion, a box of *Caran d'Ache* drawing pencils so long it would not fit in the trunk of the family's small car.

Ghislaine idolised her father, who made her a director of his football club Oxford United

But when it came to family, his generosity was circumscribed. Maxwell told his Russian mistress Kira Vladina: 'My family won't inherit anything when I die. The only ones who deserve anything are my youngest, Ghislaine, and Kevin. I adore both of them. Kevin is so much like me and Ghislaine is a friend.... The rest are a cold lot. Like their mother; and they want to live off what others earn.'

Ghislaine moved for the last two years of her secondary education to yet another exclusive school—Marlborough College, where Prince William's wife Kate Middleton would later go.

A contemporary at Marlborough school recalled her inviting a group of friends back to Headington Hall for another birthday party. Maxwell presided at the dinner and overheard Maxwell's friend swearing.

'She was summoned to the head of the table and in front of her friends dressed down by him. Everyone was saying "f***ing hell!"' they recalled. At her twenty-first-birthday party at the hall, her father turned off the electricity at 11pm because he was irritated by the guests' choice of music.

From the anorexic toddler, Ghislaine had transformed herself in her father's image. Like him she was adventurous.

As a teenager, Ghislaine was once summoned to her father's office to be asked by him: 'What's this about you nearly drowning?'

He had heard about the incident from Gianni Agnelli, the owner of the car conglomerate Fiat, whose family Ghislaine had been staying with.

'Oh, you don't mean that little accident,' replied Ghislaine. 'There was no danger.'

'You're always taking risks, doing stupid dangerous things,' Maxwell said.

'Oh Daddy,' she implored.

'I told you about jumping out of a helicopter with my skis on,' she said, insisting: 'It won't happen again.'

Ghislaine at work for her father

After Marlborough College, she joined her father's Pergamon Press at Headington Hall like her oldest brother Michael would have done, doing anything from typing to managing congresses. She had been familiar with the business set up there since she was a child as the company was based in some of the many rooms of their mansion. Ghislaine remembered her father installing the first computers at Headington in 1973.

'When I was twelve, he was already predicting the paperless office,' she recalled. 'My first job was training to use a Wang, and then programming code.'

But after nine months on staff, her father sent her

to Spain on her own to sell books and learn to fend for herself.

Ghislaine does a lucky draw working for her father

'He said go and do a useful job and come back fluent,' she said. 'I wouldn't say I did a brilliant job, but I did sell some books and came back fluent.' Later, when her father died in Spain, it meant that she would be the one of the family who could speak with the local authorities and press to deal with the aftermath.

Her father then decided she should attend Oxford University. She won a place in Modern History and Modern Languages at prestigious Balliol College, Oxford, where many former Prime Ministers of Britain had gone. Some, however, said she only got in because her father had endowed the college with the Maxwell Fellowship. This was a scholarship scheme set up by her father to fund poor students. Ghislaine's brothers' Philip and Kevin—along with Kevin's future wife Pandora—also went to Balliol which many at the university jokingly called Maxwell College. As mentioned, Boris Johnson, the current Prime Minister of Britain, attended Balliol College at the same time as she did.

At Oxford University, Ghislaine was known as 'Good Time Ghislaine'

When Ghislaine was a student, her father banned boyfriends from the house. Later in life he would vet them on the premise that any man interested in his daughter must be a gold digger. He would often tell her to dump her current beau. Determined that his favorite daughter should marry into a wealthy family, he even dreamt that she would marry John F. Kennedy Jr. In fact, at Oxford Ghislaine was the lead of a group of exclusively educated girls who proclaimed not to be interested in marrying aristocrats but rather wanted to marry into families with money.

1986, Ghislaine hugging an aristocratic friend, Diana Beaumont

A friend of actor Hugh Grant at Oxford, Ghislaine's name appeared regularly in the society columns of Britain's *Daily Mail*. She mixed with the richest and most famous people at university. As part of their initiation rites, members of the exclusive Bullingdon Club at the University of Oxford broke into the bedroom of a prospective member one night to trash it, only to find her sharing his bed. Feeling no shame, Ghislaine took the intrusion in the spirit of fun. Undaunted, she invited them in (they left, however, to trash her friend's room another time). Famous former members of the Bullingdon include recent British Prime Ministers Boris Johnson and David Cameron.

She was a bit of a Tomboy. A friend at Oxford said: 'At university whenever we went on a boys' night out, she would be the only girl with us. Guys always loved hanging out with her. She was naughty, funny and very worldly. She was as comfortable at Buckingham Palace as she was at a hip-hop convention—a chameleon who fit in everywhere.'

Prince Andrew at Tramp, 1985, one of the night clubs where Ghislaine met the returning war hero of the 1982 Falklands War and where they would take Virginia Giuffre in 2001 according to Virginia's depositions.

Yet even when she moved out of the family home and shared a house in Oxford with fellow students, she could not escape her father overbearing interest in her. On one occasion, he sent a Daimler full of Filipino servants to the house she shared with five others to tidy up, lay the table, and put a pre-cooked dinner in the oven for a party she was giving.

Compared to her siblings she was still very lucky. Elder sister Anne became an actress. After the roles dried up she went on to become a teacher. 'What have Anne and Pope John Paul II got in common?' her father would joke. 'Both are ugly and both are failed actors.' The eldest son Philip, after the death of Michael, won a scholarship to Oxford at the age of sixteen. However, after failing to join the family firm as the acolyte his father required, he moved to Argentina 'to get as far away from my father as possible,' he said. Ghislaine's twin sisters Christine and Isabel also fled the country. They moved to California where they set up an internet search business which made them close to $200 million.

Only Maxwell's youngest sons Kevin and Ian seemed to have been left as crown princes. Kevin's friends from boarding school recalled that he had to write home to his father each week, listing his achievements. They went to work for their father and ended up being prosecuted when further corporate misdeeds of their father were discovered after his death.

While at university Ghislaine had started an Oxford United supporters' club. It had 160 members and she arranged a discount for them to attend its football matches. Her father was chairman of the club and so he made her a director at the age of twenty-two. The national press immediately dubbed her 'the most attractive director in the league', a tag she didn't dispute. 'At least they're being nice about me,' she said.

Football united her with her father. At Marlborough she had played football herself in midfield for the girls' team, The Grannies, and she was seen regularly alongside her father watching the game in the directors' box. She told the interviewer that successful supporters held the key to a successful football club.

'There's more to football than watching a match. When you have a good crowd atmosphere, there is nothing better—it's electric,' she said. 'If you are enthusiastic and you can get that enthusiasm across, it acts by osmosis. You feel it. The players feel it. There are hundreds of families out there—a huge, untapped market for supporters. There are a lot of people for whom football is the core of their life. I'd like to make the club as successful as I can for their sake.'

In 1984, Maxwell took over Mirror Group Newspapers, which owned the *Daily Mirror*, then Britain's bestselling tabloid until Rupert Murdoch took over the *Sun* newspaper. Maxwell would commute from his home in Oxfordshire to the *Mirror*'s London headquarters by helicopter and Ghislaine herself later qualified as a helicopter pilot (and a deep-sea diver).

Ghislaine, director at Oxford United' football club

In 1986, she was flown out to a shipyard in The Netherlands where his new $20-million yacht, *The Lady Ghislaine* was being built and christened it with a bottle of champagne. The boat was equipped with a jacuzzi, sauna, gym and disco. He was so proud of it that he forced guests—including Donald Trump—to take their shoes off before boarding.

After university Ghislaine worked again for Pergamon for a while but then struck out on her own, finding a job in the fashion industry, though she returned to Pergamon in 1988. This time her father made her his whipping boy. She would be seen leaving his office in floods of tears after being given another dressing down, which was usually uncalled for.

While she was working as managing director of a company supplying corporate gifts her father had set up for her, she phoned him for help. She was taking a trip to New York and intended to make a business call on her father's friend Donald Trump. So she called Maxwell and asked him to phone Trump and make an appointment for her.

'Have you got a bum in your head?' yelled Maxwell. 'Why the fuck would Donald Trump want to waste his time seeing you with your crappy gifts when he has a multimillion-dollar business to run?' And he slammed down the phone. In May 1989, he himself received Trump on the *Lady Ghislaine* in New York. Trump's bigger yacht, *Trump Princess*, lay alongside and both were tickled by the fact their yachts had previously been owned by the Khashoggi family. 'He was my kind of guy', the repeat bankrupt and billionaire Trump told Larry King two years later when interviewed about the death of his friend.

Ghislaine with her father in Cannes, 1987, her mother behind them

Later when the gift company failed, he gave her a job as a columnist on his latest brainchild, *The European*, billed as 'Europe's first national newspaper,' when Maxwell himself was editor-in-chief. She could be found flying around all the European countries writing about the beautiful and the grand, and was a prominent member of the social scene. She also set up the Kit-Kat Club, an all-female debating society.

'She was very beautiful, very confident, very clever,' a friend from those days recalled, 'but she could also be quite a piece of work. You didn't want to cross her.'

A friend of Prince Andrew's called her 'clever and manipulative.' Ghislaine had known Andrew since she was at university, meeting him just when he returned from fighting in the Falklands War. Unimaginable now, Andrew was even more popular than Princess Diana, his sister in law and mother of Prince William.

'All her energy went into impressing her father, but she never quite managed it,' said a close friend. 'I went to her parents' house once and I was shocked by how hard she tried to get him to love her, notice her, to recognize her by giving her a serious job, like her brothers. But all she got, along with all she materially desired, was charity projects, social stuff.' She was her father's favorite, but she was also merely his daughter and not a son like Kevin or Ian.

Trusted Maxwell executive Nicholas Davies saw Ghislaine with her father in his office. She would hug him, slip in behind his desk and sit on his lap, cajoling him for favors—a trip to St Moritz, a new BMW, a new business venture.

'She would be affectionate,' he said, 'going up to him and kissing him on his forehead while he was sitting at his desk, calling him 'Daddy,' and he seemed, momentarily, to be genuinely pleased to see her. But if she stayed in the room for more than a few minutes Maxwell would grow impatient and want her out, suggesting she should go and leave him alone. But all the time she was in his presence Ghislaine would never be able to relax.'

Davis noted that Maxwell would blow hot and cold towards his daughter. Sometimes he liked having her around, showing her off to important guests as she was slim and beautiful. Though Maxwell had been a handsome man, over the years his culinary excesses had turned him into a bloated monster. He would often ask her to accompany him when attended lunches or dinners to entertain important guests. It was all part of what Maxwell loved most—boasting.

He bought her a lovely little house in London's Stanhope Mews and gave a black VW Gold GTi cabriolet to get around town. On other occasions he was miserly toward her. Constantly on a meager diet, she would sometimes pop into her father's kitchen in the suite to nibble on smoked salmon, cheese to take some fruit. This made her father furious and he banned her from the kitchen. His chef was instructed not to give her any food with Maxwell's express permission. Later he had the locks change to keep her out, though there were vast hordes of food kept there.

'To me it was yet another example of Maxwell's pathological need to demonstrate his power over people,' said Davies. 'He exercised it over everyone who worked for him and more so over his own family. For some extraordinary reason Maxwell had to know that he was in control over everyone at all times.'

The mews house in exclusive Belgravia Robert Maxwell gave his youngest daughter Ghislaine and where Virginia Giuffre said the infamous photograph was taken on the second floor and she had sexual relationsh with Prince Andrew. Ghislaine sold the house in 2021 to raise funds, with an asking price of $3.5 million.

Joe Haines, then a leader writer on the *Daily Mirror*, remembered her as a 'pleasant, very pretty and non-flirty young woman.' On one occasion, mistaking her for a secretary, he gave her a document to photo-copy. 'She did it without a pause,' he said.

But, like her father, she had a ruthless side. She threatened to sack a secretary because Ghislaine couldn't remember where she had parked her car. After the poor girl spent a frantic day phoning every NCP car park in London, Maxwell suddenly remembered she'd left it in the firm's underground car park.

Journalist Vassi Chamberlain first met Ghislaine Maxwell in 1990 at the opening of a restaurant in London's Soho. She recalled: 'I see a long table rammed with the deafening confidence of entitled rich young things. I sit down and immediately notice the atmosphere radiating around an attractive dark-haired girl. 'Hi, I'm Ghislaine,' she says, with an electric smile that wants you to like her. But I already know who she is: the youngest and most favored child of the publishing tycoon Robert Maxwell, an Oxford graduate and the toast of social London.'

Chamberlain was a twenty-five-year-old who had just started working in the City.

'I watched more than I spoke that night,' she said. 'Which was fine because Ghislaine barely drew breath. She was loud and great; dressed in black shorts, sheer tights and a top hat, with a touch of gold, possibly a scarf. She looked naughty and sexy, but tomboyish too, markedly at odds with the Dianaesque taffeta femininity around us. She was intriguing, an anomaly.'

Despite her outwardly gregarious and friendly demeanor there was a toughness to her, a steely implacability. A friend said: 'She was needy like a Labrador puppy. She wanted everyone to love her, always a little too much in your face, but ultimately she was focused on getting her way.' Friends say that money became her drug, the one thing that validated her existence and that she would ultimately do anything for. A need to interact with the powerful played a central role too, as did her sexual appetite.'

A younger woman who went to a party with her in London 1990 was badgered by Ghislaine into driving, even though she did not have a driver's license.

'I was so nervous but somehow she convinced me,' the woman said. 'It was a manual, so to help me as we set off, she put her hand on top of mine—but it stayed there the entire journey. If one was that way inclined, it could have been erotic, a prelude to something. But every fiber of my being was clenched with fear. It was so weird. Coerced is too strong a word. She was more a bulldozer. If she could get someone like me to do something like that, which was illegal, with that natural skill set, she was capable of anything.'

Others recalled that she had inherited some of her father's grandeur. She would ask for a cigarette and take the whole packet. 'She thought she was royalty,' one colleague recalled.

Her father's biographer Tom Bower said: 'The tragedy of Ghislaine is that she could never find a husband until she found Borgerson in her mid-fifties. She never had a steady relationship in London . It was really impossible for her. He [Maxwell] was sitting on top of her. She had no career, she had no independence.'

In the end, her father even inculcated her into his crooked ways. On November 5, 1990, Ghislaine stepped off Concorde at New York's John F Kennedy airport carrying an envelope entrusted to her by Maxwell. Inside it were nine share certificates showing the ownership of Berlitz, the international language school. Unknowingly Ghislaine had become enmeshed in a plot initiated by her father to steal $200 million from the shareholders.

Hours after Ghislaine had delivered the envelope to her father's lawyer, Kevin and Ian Maxwell authorized the re-registration of the shares from Maxwell's public company to a private company owned by the Maxwell family. The proceeds of the theft would have been enjoyed by Maxwell and his children.

After spending the day shopping in Manhattan, Ghislaine flew back to London. She was driven directly to the headquarters of Mirror Group newspapers. She handed her father another envelope that became part of Maxwell's plunder of close to $1 billion from the shareholders of his companies. At the time, Maxwell's raiding of his companies was Britain's biggest fraud in history.

1990, Ghislaine's father buys the Daily News, New York and she becomes part of Manhattan's high society.

In 1990, Maxwell took over the ailing New York *Daily News*, parking his yacht in the East River off Thirtieth Street where he served guests caviar and champagne flown in from Paris on Concorde. Otherwise he travelled the world by private jet, moving between the White House, the Kremlin, Downing Street and meeting the leaders of France, Germany, and Israel.

In the wake of her father's triumphant entrance into New York as the savior of the *Daily News*,

Ghislaine took on an important role—to be Cap'n Bob's ticket into New York society. Ghislaine was her father's escort at glittering dinners with rich and famous figures including statesman Henry Kissinger. She accompanied him to all the right parties and helped to woo the Kennedy clan. It was her that fancied the idea of her marrying John Kennedy Jnr, JFK's only son, after they had been seen kissing at a New York party. It didn't work out, but when Kerry Kennedy, daughter of assassinated Senator Robert Kennedy, was married Ghislaine was a guest.

As her father often sent Ghislaine to represent him, her circle of powerful New York friends grew and grew. At twenty-nine, she went to a dinner honoring the Nazi hunter Simon Wiesenthal and later rang her father, who was visiting President Gorbachev in Moscow, with a report of the event.

Her reward was a scathing tirade. In a written apology later, she told him: 'I am very sorry that my description of the dinner this morning was inadequate and made you angry. I should have expressed at the start of our conversation that I was merely presenting you with a preliminary report of the evening and that a full written report was to follow.' She then wrote long descriptions of every guest, praised her father and signed off: 'I will call you again tomorrow to receive your precise instructions for the Kennedy wedding.'

Her apparent lack of ambition infuriated her father. She became known as 'The Shopper.' Nevertheless, at the *Daily News*, he put her on his payroll and gave her a nebulous role in charge of 'special projects.' This provided her with another entree to Manhattan's rich and powerful.

4

MAN OVERBOARD

On the night of November 5, 1991, Robert Maxwell disappeared overboard from his yacht *The Lady Ghislaine* while cruising near the Canary Islands. It was not clear whether he had committed suicide, suffered heart attack, been murdered or simply slipped over the side. At the time his global publishing empire was burdened with debt and Maxwell had been selling assets to raise money to meet a $750 million payment due the following year. Meanwhile he was suing American journalist Seymour Hersh for alleging in a new book that he had links to Israel's Mossad spy agency. Maxwell denied that this was the case.

His sudden death left Maxwell's close associates confused. In London, Charles Wilson, director of the Mirror Group, said there had been no suggestion of foul play in the death: 'We can only assume that Mr. Maxwell slipped and fell overboard.'

Wilson also said he did not believe suicide was a

possibility. 'He had too much of the arrogance of his own ability to conceive of such a thing,' he said.

Ghislaine's father days before he disappeared from The Lady Ghislaine (behind him).

Vassi Chamberlain talked to one of her oldest friends—the person who was with Ghislaine when she first heard about her father's death and who, at her request, drove her straight to the Mirror Group offices so she could find out more about the circumstances of her father's disappearance. On the way she sobbed uncontrollably in the back seat, hidden under a blanket. She later flew out to the Canary Islands, where she declared to the media: 'I think he was murdered.'

When Ghislaine arrived on board *The Lady Ghislaine* with her mother, she was carrying $50,000 in cash to cover any expenses in cash. The *Daily Mirror* reported that Ghislaine had ordered the destruction of papers left on his yacht after her father's body had been discovered.

Reporter John Jackson said that he watched her pull papers from drawers and cabinets and throw them on the floor. She told the crew, 'I order you to shred immediately everything I have thrown on the floor,' the *Mirror* reported.

Ghislaine about to address the press surrounded by her father's crew, 7 November

She issued a statement, saying: 'I want to take this opportunity to thank all the many hundreds of people who have sent messages of support to us at this very, very sad time. I want also to thank the press for their courtesy and consideration to my mother and to us… which we appreciate very much.'

Ghislaine handled the press because she spoke

fluent Spanish and petitioned the authorities for the release of her father's body. An autopsy concluded that the cause of death was cardiovascular failure. Maxwell had been seen at his favorite spot on the starboard side of the yacht gulping for air. It would be possible for a man who had suffered a seizure, particularly one of Maxwell's heavy build, to topple over the metal cord that was the only barrier on that part of the yacht. At sixty-eight, he was hugely over-weight, with one functioning lung, fond of both his drink and his food, traveling constantly, working twenty-hour days (and sometimes more) and fighting corporate and legal battles on a dozen fronts.

Ghislaine at her father's funeral, 11 November 1991

His body was flown to Israel, accompanied by

Ghislaine, Philip, and their mother. Robert Maxwell was buried on Jerusalem's sacred Mount of Olives. Maxwell had been a major supporter of Israel and was said to be the Tel Aviv Stock Exchange's largest investor. His funeral was attended by Israeli Prime Minister Yitzhak Shamir, President Chaim Herzog, six serving and former heads of Israeli intelligence, and many dignitaries and politicians, both from the government and the opposition.

Ghislaine (middle) around the body of her father, at a service attended by the Israeli Prime Minister, President and six heads of Israeli intelligence, 11 November

Piloting Maxwell Communications Corporation's Gulfstream 4 from Jerusalem back to London that night, Captain David Whiteman was surprised by the light-hearted atmosphere in the passenger cabin. It seemed the Maxwell family had abandoned any pretense of mourning.

'It was champagne, chocolates and laughter,' Captain Whiteman recalled. 'No tears.'

It seemed that they were relieved to be rid of the tyrant and looked forward to enjoying the fortune he had amassed. Although Maxwell had loudly proclaimed that the wealth accumulated in tax-free trusts and anonymous foundations in Liechtenstein would go to charity rather than his family, they rightly believed they would not be forgotten. There were seven Liechtenstein trusts, one assigned to each of his children. Ghislaine's trust which already paid her a handsome monthly income of $10,000 through the Bank Leumi in New York. Those celebrating on the Gulfstream were content to believe that, under Kevin's stewardship of the family empire, they would receive more benefits than they had in their father's lifetime.

On the London stock exchange the value of Maxwell's master company, Maxwell Communication Corporation, was slashed by more than $500 million. Kevin Maxwell, who took over as chairman of MCC, issued a statement, admitting the company had net debts of about $2.4 billion. Ghislaine quit as a director of Oxford United Football Club which was losing $19,000 a week and had debts of $3.5 million. The club had to be sold to recoup their losses. Within six weeks Britain's Serious Fraud Office announced it would investigate an alleged scheme to prop up the value of shares in Maxwell Communication Corp. Trading in the company's shares had been suspended on December 2.

MCC had already successfully applied to a U.S. court for bankruptcy protection from creditors. An application was made in the High Court in London to put the company's British assets into administration. Maxwell's publishing empire collapsed with $4.4 billion of debt. Kevin Maxwell was declared bankrupt with debts of $650 million. It was then discovered that the share price had been propped up by looting the company's pension fund, leaving employees without pensions. In 1995, Kevin, Ian, and two other former directors went on trial for conspiracy to defraud, but were unanimously acquitted by a twelve-man jury in 1996. When it was all done dusted up to $1 billion remained unaccounted for.

Ghislaine did not recover well from her father's death.

'She was catatonic. It hit her in a way that scared people. She hit absolute rock bottom, she didn't stop crying,' said friend. 'It must have been so complicated for her. All the security she had grown up with. She was the life and soul of the party wherever she wanted to go in the world and never had to worry about money.'

While the Maxwell brothers had troubles of their own, *Vanity Fair* found Elisabeth Maxwell still living in Headington Hall, but with no staff or chauffeur-driven Bentley.

'I'm in great financial difficulty,' she told the magazine. 'They've stopped my pension. I haven't salted anything away, because I never for a minute believed that he'd leave me destitute. They say I have £500,000 [$850,000]. Those are lies. I haven't anything. It wasn't my way, of spiriting things away. Anyway, I didn't have access to funds.'

While two maids had been laid off, she nonetheless retained a Filipino cook and housekeeper.

The furniture and *objets d'art* were deemed to be her private property. Then there was a chateau in France bought last summer with a $5 million loan from a company controlled by Ian and Kevin and so was also possibly outside the grasp of administrators. It also emerged that she had given $1.5 million of her own money to help pay for Kevin and Ian's enormous legal fees in defending their position before the House of Commons select committee, where they refused to answer any questions. Kevin and Ian lived in houses jointly owned with their wives, so little of their asset value would be returned to MGN pensioners. Eventually financial losses forced Mrs

Maxwell to auction her personal belongings and move into a borrowed apartment in London.

After her father's death, Ghislaine fled to the US where she was soon seen in the circle of Texas millionaire Steven Wyatt, then thought to be the lover of the Duchess of York.

Ghislaine in mourning in New York, November 1991

Even after his death and fraudulent acts, the twenty-nine-year-old still rode to the defense of her father.

'He wasn't a crook,' she said. 'I'm surviving—just. But I can't just die quietly in a corner. I have to believe that something good will come out of this mess. It's sad for my mother. It's sad to have lost my dad. It's sad for my brothers. But I would say we'll be back. Watch this space.'

New Yorker Helen Kirwan-Taylor said that it was in particular Ghislaine's friendship with Prince Andrew helped her in the US.

'Ghislaine came over with the stamp of approval from Prince Andrew,' she said. 'The thinking was if she hangs out with him, she must be OK.'

Being British helped too.

'I observed how easy it was for someone with a British accent and the faint whiff of poshness to forge their way into the most exclusive circles. *Brideshead Revisited* [a bit like *Downton Abbey* now] had captured the nation's imagination,' she recalled. Brits 'managed to infiltrate every circle, appearing at all the right parties and nightclubs.'

Kirwan-Taylor was among the list of prominent people in the little black book of contacts that Maxwell later curated for Jeffery Epstein.

'Ghislaine was like a sniffer dog: sharp, alert and with a nose that could detect any useful information,' she said. 'I was then an assistant producer at *60 Minutes* with access to presidents and prime ministers;

that caught her attention. I remember her as being quick-witted, attention-seeking and the complete darling of her set. She appeared at every party along with half a dozen of the then-It girls whose main occupation seemed to be finding a wealthy man with a 'house.' Ghislaine's close female friends, however, were career-minded and independent as she clearly was.'

However, Maxwell's only career seems to have been mixing in the social whirl.

'Not only was she mixing with the very rich, but she seemed to be right in the middle of the action. In fact, she seemed to be directing traffic. Socializing was her clearly well-paid job,' said Kirwan-Taylor.

Another friend described why she became so popular in New York: 'She is great fun, highly intelligent and always wants to meet new people and do interesting things.'

Ghislaine was then living in an apartment overlooking Central Park in New York owned by an Iranian friend, though she retained her Kensington mews house in London, then valued at $550,000. She ostensibly worked for an upmarket real estate office on Madison Avenue, but spent her time socializing with a crowd that included Ivana Trump and billionaire arms dealer Adnan Khashoggi's son. Although she no longer had any connection with the corporate gift company her father had helped her set up, there were questions about the alleged payment of $800,000 to her when he bought the company back—particularly from those who had been left without a pension following the collapse of his empire.

Ghislaine occasionally made trips back to Britain on Concorde, though was said to have worn a white wig to conceal her identity on the streets of London. A one-way trip on Concorde costs more than $3,000—a lot of money for a young woman reported to be living on a 'meager' $100,000 a year from the trust fund set up by her father.

When her father was still alive, she would scoop up job lots of twenty or thirty return tickets on Concorde at $10,000 a time so she could flit back and forth at will. But she failed to note that they had an expiry date. This became apparent when she was seen waving a wad around in an airline office, where she was told that she should consult the travel agent who had issued them.

'Oh I don't think I can do that,' said a crestfallen Ghislaine, turning on her heels and walking out. The travel agent had gone bust.

Vassi Chamberlain caught up with Ghislaine again in New York in 1992 at a party in a downtown loft, not long after her father's death. She said: 'Ghislaine looked unkempt, shell-shocked, vibrating with anger and bitterness. Talking to her was hard work. It was not clear whether she had met Epstein by this point, but she was quick to mention that she was living in some style on the Upper East Side. I remember thinking, but with what money?'

In fact, Jeffery Epstein had already arrived on the scene at this low point in Ghislaine's life. He was an associate of her father's and they first met at a memorial held in New York hosted by the actor Tony Randall.

24 November 1991, Ghislaine meets her father's associate Jeffrey Epstein at a memorial hosted by Tony Randall

Before her father died, Ghislaine had split from her great love, Count Gianfranco Cicogna. A dashing member of the Ciga hotels clan, Cicogna was the man who molded Ghislaine's image like her father had before him. He told her where to get her hair cut and what to wear. Their affair lasted for four years and finished when he replaced her TV weathergirl Tania Bryer. He died in a blazing crash at an airshow in South Africa in 2012.

Money was getting tight despite what Ghislaine said. She was soon living in a $500-a-week one-bedroom apartment on the Upper East Side close to Epstein's home, but then she was reported to have moved to an even cheaper studio apartment.

Ghislaine dating actor George Hamilton at the Derby, Epsom, 1991

In 1991, Ghislaine was still dating actor George Hamilton when they attended the Derby together. But, then, Epstein accompanied her to a restaurant opening in Manhattan where Ghislaine was billed as the 'celebrity' invitee. She was also a regular guest at his Upper East Side apartment. The *Mail on Sunday* in Britain rushed out an article headlined 'The Mystery of Ghislaine Maxwell's Secret Love.'

Little was known about Epstein at the time, except that in 1980 he had been nominated as *Cosmopolitan* magazine's 'Bachelor of the Month.' His telephone number was listed under the name 'Jeffrey Edwards'. The door bell at his home on East 69th Street simply carried the initials 'J.E.' Any request to speak to him was met with the reply from a male voice: 'He may be here, or he may not. Who wants to know?'

One story linked him to the CIA and, like Maxwell's father, to the Mossad. Another was that he was a math teacher at an exclusive girls school. Indeed he had been a math teacher at one time at the school of one of Murdoch's daughters and also of Trump's Attorney General William Barr, before moving to Wall Street. Close to the mark was that he was a corporate spy hired by big businesses to recover money that had been embezzled.

It was noted that his social rise has been accompanied by a remorseless attraction to well-connected, rich, and beautiful women. One of his first notable dates was Nikki Haskell, a former TV talk-show hostess who met him in 1986. Haskell was then giving some of the most prominent parties in New York, and Epstein, who lived close by, became a regular guest.

'Jeffrey didn't talk about his past, although he claimed to have been a concert pianist,' she said.

Epstein escorted Haskell to the annual BEST Awards in New York, a glamorous event celebrating the most fashionable people in America. Haskell said: 'In the middle, Jeffrey got up and said 'I have to go'. When I asked why, he said: 'Just look at me as a doctor who has to make a house call.' Who was he meeting at midnight on a Saturday?'

'Jeffrey is the type of person whose stories sound far-fetched, but you never know when you will run into him,' said New York socialite Dorothy Sowell. 'There is something about him that must ring true.'

Epstein told Sowell that he had once been a stockbroker and investment banker for Bear Stearns, but the National Association of Securities Dealers has no record of him with that company. According to friends, Epstein was born and raised in Coney Island, New York. His parents were relatively poor, but then lived in a house he bought for them in Palm Beach, Florida.

His Madison Avenue office was decorated with fabulous works of art, and he has been known to drive a Silver Spirit Rolls-Royce. He appeared to have an inexhaustible supply of money, yet no one seemed to know where it had come from.

Epstein became the right-hand man of Leslie

Wexner, the founder of the Limited Corporation, a giant retailing chain which bought underwear company Victoria's Secret in 1982.

Ghislaine's New York friends were very supportive of her relationship with Epstein. They saw in the eight-year older billionaire a new father figure for her. Indeed, those who knew Robert Maxwell were struck by the similarity of character between the two men and their approach to their extraordinary wealth.

Epstein's office

Briefly she and Epstein were an item. According to a profile in *Vanity Fair*, Epstein was not one for long-term romantic relationships but 'he tells people that when a relationship is over, the girlfriend "moves up, not down" to friendship status.'

This was how the next step of their relationship unfolded. Epstein's money opened doors but he did not have much of a social life, which is where Ghislaine stepped in. He said that Ghislaine was not on his payroll but organized much of his life and was his 'best friend.'

'Jeff took her in and when she felt better she looked around and realized he could replace the lifestyle she had had—and what a lifestyle it was,' said a friend. 'She could go back to doing whatever she wanted. Previously the price of that had been having her father. Now the price was this guy. What they both enabled her to do was be herself. She could go off and be this madcap spirit.'

A source who knew her late father said: 'Having a dominant bully like Robert Maxwell as a father may well have given her a taste for similar men, and driven her into the arms of Epstein.'

The dynamic was that Ghislaine organized a life that revolved around Epstein's nine-floor mansion on Manhattan's Upper East Side (believed to be the biggest private residence in the city), a vast ranch in New Mexico called Zorro, and his private island in the Caribbean.

There was even talk of them moving in together. Although this did not come to fruition, she held a launch party for her mother's book, *A Mind of My*

Own: My Life with Robert Maxwell (1994) there. In a speech at the party, Betty blamed her husband's plundering of the employees' pension funds of his companies and subsequent downfall on anti-semitism in Britain. 'Things would have been different if Bob had lived in America,' she thought.

No US publisher was interested, however, in a 536-page about the unknown Betty until she asked Rupert Murdoch for advice and his company HarperCollins US agreed to publish her. In it she detailed how, in the last decade of his life, as her husband's behavior grew progressively more eccentric and cruel, yet she remained loyal, despite his prolonged absences, womanizing and repeated threats of a legal separation. Over the hundreds of pages of the massive tome about her life, there were less than a handful of fleeting references to Ghislaine.

By then Ghislaine seemed to organize even the most seemingly trivial aspects of Epstein's life. In 1993, an advertisement appeared in *Yoga Journal* seeking a yoga instructor for 'a private individual' with 'fantastic perks such as extensive travel.' The number listed was that of Epstein's office. Those interested in the job were told to call 'Miss Maxwell' there.

According to journalist and author Wendy Leigh, who also knew Robert Maxwell, Ghislaine's 'social cachet primarily derives from her contact with Prince Andrew and her willingness to show up for any fashion or beauty-related events. Celebrating the opening of a Manhattan store is one of Ghislaine's specialities. Where Ivana Trump, Joan Collins and Denise Rich rub shoulders, you will find Ghislaine. At an event to support the New York City Opera Thrift Shop she bought a pink velvet Dolce & Gabbana coat. She was spotted at a party thrown by Christie Hefner at the *Playboy* penthouse on Fifth Avenue where bunny girls served drinks and a drag act performed.'

Her own parties were well attended. At one, in honor of Allegra Hicks, whose husband, Ashley, is the grandson of Lord Mountbatten, the eighty guests included Hollywood star Matthew Modine, the Kennedy family member and TV personality Carole Radziwill, the PR guru Peggy Siegal, and the socialite Julie Janklow, as well as a Rockefeller, along with a good sprinkling of countesses and Manhattan billion-aires.

Wendy Leigh believed that the key to understanding Ghislaine's relationship with Epstein was her love for her domineering father.

'Her desperation to please him, to live up to his high standard of success at all costs, must surely haunt her, even years after his death,' Leigh said.

'How did Ghislaine manage to conquer the heights of Manhattan society, both salubrious and not so salubrious? The secret, I believe, is that she was always daddy's girl, and thought that she was entitled to mingle only with the best. Thus armed with self-confidence and Maxwell's favorite motto ('kindness, courtesy and consideration'[*sic*]) she effortlessly charmed her way to the top.'

Epstein and Donald Trump in November 1992, a year after Epstein met Ghislaine.

Vassi Chamberlain, who caught up with her again, said: 'Ghislaine was, by all accounts, a complicated person; a seductive blend of charm and guile; a schemer, always working at full tilt, having traded one depraved master for another.'

A New Yorker who got to know Ghislaine through his ex-girlfriend, called her 'a modern-day geisha girl of the capitalist world. She inhabits a domain filled with the richest people in the world—some of whom are good guys, and some of whom are bad—and who think they are above the law. It's a world frequented by young half-naked girls in bikinis, billionaires and lavish lifestyles, but it borders on the grotesque. You are never really sure what is going on behind closed doors.'

Another said: 'She spoke the language of men.' On a more personal level, he added: 'Ghislaine is charming, sexy and off-the-scale flirtatious. When I met her, I thought, 'Are we going to f***?' Unlike many English girls who I see move to New York, and marry millionaires and live the high life, Ghislaine seems subservient to men. She wants to belong in a man's world and make herself indispensable to it. I'm sure it all goes back to having a bully of a father and being overshadowed by strong brothers. She wants to please, and those around her want to be pleased. It's a pretty straightforward kind of deal.'

Another New Yorker who knew her extremely well and went to dinner at Epstein's Manhattan townhouse, put it more bluntly: 'She would not have been unique in being someone who lives well and possesses a sexual peccadillo of sharing women with her boyfriend. Underlying all of this was her libertarian sexual appetite.'

How she met Epstein is unclear. One theory is that Epstein had business dealings with her father and that was the reason she decamped to New York after he died.

'My personal belief is that Epstein had been hiding money siphoned off by Robert Maxwell,' said one New Yorker, who knew Epstein before Ghislaine turned up in New York. 'Jeffrey was always very mysterious, and for years the only client he had was the Victoria's Secret owner, Leslie Wexner. The point is, Jeffrey was never a money manager. What he did was structure offshore funds, not to manage them but to hide or recover money. I believe it was Jeffrey who laundered Maxwell's money. I couldn't work out at first how, the second Ghislaine landed in New York, she was all of a sudden—overnight really—very chummy with Jeffrey. Then he started spending on a different level, suddenly buying these extraordinary townhouses.'

He was skeptical about their relationship and believed that there was never a romantic relationship between them, rather a relationship based on money.

'I can't tell you how many times I said to Ghislaine, "I hear Jeffrey's bought a house in Palm Beach." She would say, "Darling, that's my house." I could never figure out why Ghislaine always acted like a boss towards him. I believe they had a business arrangement from day one. For a start he would never have been attracted to her. We know the kind of girls he liked. Also, why would she have been so interested in procuring girls for him? No girlfriend does that.'

He remembered Ghislaine asking him about a beautiful Russian redhead he knew. 'Ghislaine said to me, 'That girl is very pretty, you should introduce her to Jeffrey.' She was his wing-woman from day one. She went to New York to see Jeffrey, she didn't go and then meet Jeffrey.'

A British couple who stayed with Ghislaine in New York after she met Epstein were also surprised by her extravagant life and the size of her Manhattan townhouse.

'My first thought was, how did she afford this?' said the wife. 'I asked her about her work and she was adamant that she'd earned it all herself, that it was her money. I tried to get to the bottom of it, but she was quite vague.'

While they were staying, Ghislaine threw a dinner party. Guests included Prince Andrew and two Oscar-winning actresses who played virtual games on the huge movie screen in the basement. The next night they ate in a local restaurant where, they were told, Andrew would be joining them.

'I remember seeing him sitting at a table at the far end with these three young blonde girls when we walked in,' the wife said. 'He immediately got up, I imagined to join us, but instead he said goodbye and left with them in tow. It was all very strange.'

Ghislaine, Epstein and Lynn Forester in 1995: two years later Forester bought 116 E 65th St she would sell to Ghislaine in 2000. It sold in 2015 for $15 million.

Others also observed that, with Epstein, Ghislaine was the boss. Christopher Mason, a British contributor to *The New York Times* known for the musical 'roasts' he wrote and performed, recalled being hired by Ghislaine to write a song for Epstein's birthday.

'Normally I speak to as many people who know the person as possible,' he said. 'But this time I was only allowed to speak to Ghislaine.'

He was told that one line had to include how

Epstein had been the object of schoolgirl crushes at Dalton, the private Upper East Side school where he had worked as a math teacher from 1974 to 1976. Another should mention his twenty-four-hour erections.

Another old friend summed up the situation: 'There was some kind of toxic control going on, a lifestyle she felt she deserved and in exchange she made a Faustian pact with Epstein that ultimately compromised any morals she might have had. She had a choice to remain the Ghislaine we all knew and loved, or become the other, for money and power. She chose the latter.'

In Manhattan she went out every night, being seen at every cocktail party and charity dinner, every restaurant in a relentless assault on the rich and powerful.

'She was very well connected and went around with a rarefied air,' said Candace Bushnell, the author of *Sex and the City*. 'She name-dropped this person and that person, so you always knew where you were in terms of status.'

There was a widely circulated rumor that she had an affair with Bill Clinton at the time.

'Of course I heard about it, and it wouldn't take a leap of faith to imagine it happened,' said a senior member of London's international business community. A spokesman for Clinton said: 'It's a total lie today, it's a total lie tomorrow and it'll be a total lie years from now.'

Bushnell thought a part of the power Ghislaine wielded was her ability to deal with tough, shady men. Because her father was a crook, such men seemed normal to her. 'She knew what to say to them, and a lot of women don't because there's always an under-lying sexual thing going on, a vibe of sex. There are a lot of sleazy people in high positions everywhere, you have to look out for them. But once you engage in that world, you are sucked in. She got sucked in.'

Maxwell introduced Epstein to girls she knew in Manhattan who worked at places such as Sotheby's. Many went on trips to Epstein's houses, and their names appear in flight logs. Later she, allegedly according to the Manhattan US Attorney, supplied more vulnerable girls who were younger and more malleable. Meanwhile she lived the highlife.

'Whenever I saw Ghislaine, she was either leaving New York or on her way back from somewhere fab-ulous,' said Bushnell. 'It all sounded rather grand, but also so believable. She had the perfect backstory, so no one questioned it.'

Ghislaine went skiing in Aspen, when celebrities such as Barbara Streisand and Martina Navratilova boycotted the resort after Colorado restricted the rights of same-sex couples. At a sixties' party in Palm Beach, she was seen doing a 'scarf dance.'

Ghislaine and Epstein attend the New York premiere of Batman Forever, 1995 (four federal sex trafficking charges cover the years 1994-1997).

And she was seen at parties and at the opening of celebrity restaurants in both New York and London, brushing shoulders with the likes of heiress Ariadne Beaumont, banker Ron Perelman, said to be New York's richest man, Mort Zuckerman, then owner of the *Daily News*, Jacqui Kennedy's sister Princess Lee Radziwill, and in England with British top-impresario Lord Grade, the leading Irish comedian Dave Allen, and celebrity photographer Terry O'Neill. At the premiere of *Batman Forever* she was seen with movie stars Michael Douglas and Tatum O'Neal. At Pravda, New

York's hottest nightspot, she was seen with old Oxford friend Hugh Grant.

Maxwell was guest of honor at a Christmas party given by Australian trucking magnate Lindsay Fox on the hundred-foot yacht in Sydney Harbor. Epstein accompanied her. They were thought to have spent Christmas on the exclusive Lizard Island, a luxury resort on the Great Barrier Reef. Some thought it bad taste taking Ghislaine out on the harbor after what had happened to her father, but one of the guests pointed out: 'You can't visit Sydney and not go out on the Harbor—it's like going to Paris and avoiding the Eiffel Tower.'

The Sydney *Sun Herald* reported that Ghislaine had by this time publicly distanced herself from her two bankrupted brothers, Kevin and Ian, but was said to be a 'loyal supporter of her late father, Cap'n Bob.'

5

'THE COOLEST PERSON ALIVE'

By the mid-1990s, *The Times* listed Ghislaine as one of the 'Britons who matter in Manhattan.' At the time British women were taking over as editors of American magazines. She was said to be one of 'thirty-something spinsters... breaking hearts for England.' It was in 1995 that Epstein and she first met Maria and Annie Farmer, the artist and her high-school going sister who were to become one of the first known accusers of the pair.

In 1996, Maxwell took aim in the press at the mass-market novelist Jeffrey Archer to protect the reputation of her father. Archer's latest bestseller *Fourth Estate* was based on the rise and fall of her father. She had not read it, but this didn't deter her from criticizing the book.

'Why bother?' she said. 'It's fiction just like the earlier "biographies" which purported to be nonfiction.'

She added mischievously that it's no surprise that Archer's Rupert Murdoch-type character emerges a hero: 'Murdoch is publishing his book.' Rupert Murdoch was her father's great rival on both sides of the Atlantic and, two years before, HarperCollins US had also published her mother's deeply critical memoir of her father.

Ghislaine in 1996 (four federal sex trafficking charges cover the years 1994-1997).

The outburst took place at a Fashion Cafe party for *Verve* magazine, just launched by India's Mahindra family. Hosting the bash was model India Hicks, granddaughter of India's last viceroy, Lord Mountbatten. Among the guests were Knopf's top editor Sonny Mehta and actress Sigourney Weaver.

Archer struck back in London at the Kit-Kat

Club, Ghislaine's all-female debating society.

'I had the time of my life, surrounded by women under forty,' he wrote afterward, trying to beat her at her own game. 'I had orgasm after orgasm just talking to them!'

But the socializing took its toll when she was stopped in Fulham, West London, driving her E-reg Golf GTI without lights at 4.30am. After she was arrested, she treated tired traffic police to tea and biscuits and a flick through the family photographs at her brother's home. She had taken the officers to her brother's home in order to prove she had a British address. After being bailed by police, she went back to the US, later returning to England for the court hearing.

When she appeared before Horseferry Road Magistrates on August 9, 1996 on a drunk-driving charge she gave her occupation as 'internet writer' and said she was 'of no fixed abode.' Defense lawyer Keith Oliver put it to the court she was a woman 'of moderate means' based in New York. Maxwell joked she was 'allergic' to booze, but admitted being 1½ times over the legal limit. She was given a year's driving ban and a £1,000 fine, plus £75 costs.

Back in New York, Maxwell had established herself as the go-to Brit for celebrity events. She stood in for the Duchess of York, Prince Andrew's wife, at the Asian Art Fair, where twenty of the fifty exhibitors were from London. Breathlessly, the gossip columns reported that the svelte Ghislaine resisted the lentil curry canapes, explaining: 'My skirt will burst if I do.'

Backing her credentials as a super-Brit, she was seen at the Alfred Dunhill Queen's Cup polo final at Smith's Lawn, Windsor Great Park, where the Queen presented the prizes. Maxwell wore sunglasses throughout in spite of a thunderstorm. She told *The Times* that reports she was engaged were baloney, but refused to disclose where she was currently working, if at all. The paper said she had 'the chameleon career profile of the serial socializer, and is variously reported to be into real estate, interior design, party planning and charity work. A fully fledged DGW: daughter/girlfriend/whatever.'

That October 1997, she was at the Ford Models fiftieth-anniversary party, which Donald Trump allegedly gate-crashed. Having failed once through her father, this time beautiful thirty-something black-haired Ghislaine tried to engage him in conversation but he could not take his eyes off the blond models in their mid-twenties. The season continued with a round of parties in Palm Beach and New York. She joined then 'It Girl' Nina Griscom jumping off a diving board at the *Inside Sports'* Swimsuit Issue bash.

Ghislaine modelling vintage clothing for Sotheby's 1999.

But Ghislaine was rarely seen in public with Epstein. 'That's because he was a con artist who operated in this enormous house with its hidden caves—everything happened in that house,' said another Manhattan stalwart, who once attended a dinner in Epstein's mansion. 'For the men it was, like, 'Come to my house and I'll give you some candy.' I

108

was out seven nights a week and I never saw him once.' Ghislaine on the other hand entertained lavishly in her new townhouse. 'It was very dark and she would have these parties, always dressed in a ridiculous sexy-at-home outfit. I remember thinking, what am I doing here, she's creepy.'

Yet behind the scenes introductions were made. In Nassau, the Bahamas, Epstein 'met Princess Sarah Ferguson and kids on the ground' in April 16 1998. Ghislaine had opened the door to Epstein's friendship with Prince Andrew.

Although the Duke was voted top dinner party guest in *Tatler*, Andrew is not renowned for his sparkling conversation: 'However, that won't deter ambitious social climbers, including Ghislaine Maxwell. Those who read *Tatler* would overlook such things for the privilege of having a real live Royal prince at their table.'

They then turned up together at a Ralph Lauren fashion show. Andrew was on leave from the Royal Navy at the time, and a year later he would retire from active service. They met the models backstage afterwards. There was no hint of a relationship between Andrew and Ghislaine. At the time it was rumored that he was seeing Wonderbra model Caprice, though he was actually dating twenty-three-year-old French professional golfer Audrey Rimbault, who he sneaked into Buckingham Palace for a tour of his private quarters. Then Ghislaine introduced him to Australian PR girl Emma Gibbs. He was said to be 'head over heels in love' and even stayed at her New York home for a week. As with Epstein, she seemed to be making introductions for her close male friends.

Ghislaine and Prince Andrew at the wedding of Aurelia Cecil, a mutual friend, 2000.

'Andrew is very, very keen on Emma,' said the *Sun*. 'Although she's slightly less struck, they have been seeing a lot of each other. She's in her early thirties and is very attractive and bubbly. And, crucially, she laughs at all his awful jokes!'

But Ghislaine was never far away. The couple were spotted dining together in New York in April

2000, causing some newspapers to speculate they were dating as they were spotted so often together. And there was continued talk that Andrew and Fergie would remarry, while he and Ghislaine were 'just good friends.' She had been his closest confidante since the Yorks' breakup. Nevertheless they tried to avoid the prying lenses of photographers after lunch at Nello's on Madison Avenue on April 20, 2000.

The New York *Post* called this a 'lovey-dovey lunch' and Ghislaparisine his 'sweetheart.'

'Sarah Ferguson's former hubby held hands with his new love and was seen eating a meal of salad and chops,' the paper continued. 'But the dashing prince—once known as Randy Andy for his escapades with sexy film star Koo Stark—was apparently eager to keep his latest romance under wraps.'

The *Sun* said they ate a $120 lobster, rather than chops and salad. 'After lunch, Ghislaine—daughter of late media tycoon Robert Maxwell—exited by herself, leaving Andrew to settle the bill. Next, Andrew walked out and immediately pulled a cell phone from his jacket. Ghislaine was window-shopping down the street, a witness said.

'When Andy spotted our photographer, Ghislaine quickly ran into a shop, occasionally peering out to see if the coast was clear. The two eventually abandoned their plan to reunite on

Madison Avenue and met up later,' the witness said.'

Other papers made more of this and photographer Lawrence Schwartzwald said: 'Andrew was like a gentleman caught with his pants down. At one stage, he tried to hide behind some shrubbery.'

A member of staff at Nello's said: 'They were more into each other than the food. It was wonderful to watch. Ghislaine is a great girl. She comes in here all the time. Prince Andrew has been here before—last year with Ghislaine.'

The news got back to Buckingham Palace where courtiers were said to fear that Andrew was heading for another failed romance. One said: 'I don't think the daughter of Robert Maxwell would be very suitable.'

Of course, Ghislaine was at the opening party of businessman and Formula-One team owner Flavio Briatore's exclusive new club, The Billionaire, in Sardinia. Also on hand were Davinia Taylor, Naomi Campbell, the Italian football stars Francesco Totti and Filippo Inzaghi, Chelsea's Gianluca Vialli, restaurateur Mogens Tholstrup, race driver Eddie Irvine, the fashion designer Roberto Cavalli, the Benetton driver Giancarlo Fisichella, and Fergie.

Briatore claimed: 'We have the highest concentration of the most beautiful girls anywhere in Europe.'

You had to be a friend of Briatore to get in and

champagne was $200–$900 a bottle. Ghislaine was also pictured with trendspotting hotelier Andre Balazs, owner of Chateau Marmont and The Standard on Sunset Boulevard in L.A., the Mercer Hotel in Manhattan and Sunset Beach on Shelter Island. The European-born husband of Ford Models Katie Ford was bringing a version of The Standard to Downtown Manhattan. It was followed shortly after in May by Briatore's birthday party for his girlfriend Naomi in St Tropez's harbor. Ghislaine had brought the sixteen year old Virginia.

Ghislaine and Virginia in St Tropez harbour, May 2000.

Irvine said he attended one of Epstein's parties where he saw Ghislaine Maxwell with Virginia Roberts Giuffre. Bill Clinton was also there.

Ghislaine with Virginia in St Tropez, May 2000.

In June 2000, Ghislaine was so close to Prince Andrew that she got an invitation to the 'Dance of the Decade', marking Andrew's fortieth birthday, the Queen Mother's hundredth, Princess Margaret's seventieth and Princess Anne's fiftieth. It was hosted by the Queen at Windsor Castle. Maxwell attended with Epstein. It was Andrew's last year in the navy, a year later he would travel the world as UK trade envoy.

As Andrew saw more and more of Ghislaine, so did the prince's relationship with Epstein grow ever closer and closer. Over their twelve-year acquaintance, Andrew stayed with Epstein at his various residences, sometimes spending days on end with him. Epstein meanwhile was also in contact with Fergie, speaking regularly on the phone, and bailing her out with his money.

The flight log for Epstein's private jet, later dubbed 'the Lolita Express', showed 'Prince Andrew' in flight records for the first time in February 1999, flying into the Virgin Islands. A few days later, he flew out again with 'JE'—Jeffrey Epstein; 'GM'—Ghislaine Maxwell and a number of other people.

Only a few months later, in April 1999, Prince Andrew attended as guest of honor a private dinner party hosted by Maxwell at Epstein's New York townhouse. Also present at the intimate dinner were billionaires Ronald Perelman, Donald Trump and Mort Zuckerman. Reciprocating the friendship, Andrew welcomed Epstein and a group of young women at the Queen's private estate in Scotland, Balmoral, some months later.

The friendship was to remain strong for a very long time. Andrew flew on Epstein's private jet from Luton to Edinburgh with Ghislaine Maxwell on September 1, 2006, six weeks after Epstein had been arrested on charges of soliciting prostitution in Florida in July. This followed on from Ghislaine, Epstein and Harvey Weinstein's attendance at Andrew's oldest daughter Princess Beatrice's 18th birthday ball at Windsor Castle as his guests. This was only days after Epstein's release on bail after his arrest in Florida.

In September 2000, Andrew and Ghislaine arrived separately at the wedding of his old flame Aurelia Cecil to restaurant owner Rupert Stephenson at the parish church of St Michael in Compton Chamberlayne in Salisbury, Wiltshire. But they left together and joined other guests at a dinner and dance. She was wearing a strapless black-and-white checked dress. Earlier, in February 2000, Maxwell, Epstein and Prince Andrew were again seen publicly with Donald Trump and Melania at his Mar-al-Lago estate for a celebrity tennis tournament.

Donald Trump, Melania, Prince Andrew, Epstein and Ghislaine (far right), Mar-a-Lago February 2000.

In October 2000, Andrew was seen with Maxwell and Epstein at Victoria's Secret model Heidi Klum's S&M-themed Halloween party at Manhattan's Hudson Bar. An uncostumed Donald Trump, sporting a red lip print on his forehead from one of Klum's kisses, brought his new squeeze Melania Knauss, who would become his third wife.

Donald Trump, Melania, and Ghislaine at Heidi Klum's Halloween Party.

At one point Andrew staggered to his feet and headed towards the dance floor. He stood clutching a rail around the dance area with both hands while Maxwell, who was dressed as a prostitute in tight gold trousers and a blonde wig, put her arm around him. While the prince's bodyguards looked on from a safe distance, Maxwell said: 'I'm a hooker tonight. We are going on to another party with a pimps-and-prosti-tutes theme.'

A friend of Fergie's said: 'There is no doubt his antics have caused the Duchess of York to raise her eyebrows to the heavens. I doubt if she will be pleased at hearing of his night out in New York with Ghislaine.

Ghislaine and Prince Andrew at Heidi Klum's Halloween Party, 2000

'The Duchess is very protective of her two daughters—as Andrew is—and she will be concerned about his image as a caring father in their eyes. She is sure to ask whether it is the right image for the girls, to see their dad out until all hours with a strange collection of people dressed in black PVC and dog collars.'

They went on to the trendy Lotus supper club. The source said: 'He always sees Ghislaine when he is in New York.'

A week after the party, her oversized Jeep drew up outside the Nag's Head pub in the heart of London's Belgravia village. At the wheel was a razor-thin Ghislaine, dressed down but chic in jeans and a sweatshirt. Her face was scrubbed free of make-up and her dark hair was tucked under that distinctive trademark of her late father—a New York Yankees baseball cap.

In that part of town where celebrities and royalty pass unnoticed, locals were unfazed by the brief appearances of occasional resident Ghislaine Maxwell at the mews house her father had bought her. They looked on amused as she swigged from a bottle of beer as she flirted with the barman, oblivious to the traffic building up behind her in the narrow cobbled street.

An American friend said: 'The reason she has men eating out of her hand is she manages to make them feel sexy and fascinating. She's an outrageous flirt and fascinated by dodgy, powerful men. It's all part of her Electra complex.'

In charge of her own palace, London's *Sunday Times* was called her the queen of the transatlantic set, though her life was as secretive as her father's.

Clocking up countless air miles, she was seen as the ruler of what *Newsweek* identified as the NY-LON Society. The only competition was actress Liz Hurley and model Sophie Dahl. In London though, her father's name was still a burden, while in New York, she had found that she could do as she pleased without fear of censure.

As her long-time friend Elizabeth Saltzman, the fashion director of *Vanity Fair*, said: 'New York gave her the freedom to go ahead and be creative whether it was in business or socially. Ghislaine's fun, she's energetic and she makes things happen. She's a people gatherer, but she's no bimbo. She's a smart operator with a huge intellect and people in New York respect her for that.'

The *Sunday Times* went on: 'Yet, for all her high-profile appearances on Manhattan's A-list merry-go round, she is secretive to the point of paranoia and her business affairs are deeply mysterious.'

Her relationship with Epstein was also shrouded in mystery, even for Manhattan's cognoscenti. 'He's Mr Enigmatic. Nobody knows whether he's a concert pianist, property developer, a CIA agent, a math teacher or a member of Mossad,' said a New York social observer. 'Jeffrey provides some financial support and he's always kept her secrets, but nobody knows what their relationship is really about.'

By now Ghislaine was said to be worth $30 million. Her father's yacht, *The Lady Ghislaine*, which had been bought by a Saudi and renamed *The Lady Mona K*, was back on sale for $50 million.

Ghislaine's NY opulent mansion 116E 65th St, purchased through an anonymous company linked to Epstein

It was also in the whirlwind year 2000 of Prince Andrew and Epstein that Ghislaine moved into her own monumental 7,000-square-foot townhouse at 116 East 65th Street—less than ten blocks from Epstein's mansion. mansion 11 minutes around the corner from Epstein on 116 East 65th Street. It was bought for $4.495 million by limited liability company, with an address that matches the office of J. Epstein & Co. Representing the buyer was Darren Indyke, Epstein's longtime lawyer.

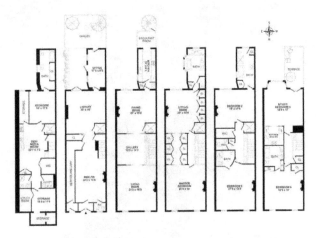

The floor plan of Ghislaine Maxwell's NY mansion 116E 65th St.

Interestingly, this was $20,000 less that the amount for which vendor Lynn Forester—Epstein and Maxwell's friend as well as the Clintons and, a month later, wife of British financier Evelyn de Rothchild—had bought the property in 1997. It was also close to $10 million less than the market value in 2000. Fifteen years later, Maxwell cashed in on the windfall. Months after being sued by Epstein victim Virginia Giuffre for defamation, she put her stylish house on the market for $18.995 million.

The Beaux-Arts-style property from 1910 lay between Park and Lexington Avenues, had twelve rooms, including six bedrooms; nine wood-burning fireplaces; an elevator; a media room and library with built-in projector and Surround Sound; a home office; a chef's kitchen with granite countertops, and a garden. It had a twenty-foot frontage on 65th Street, against Epstein's mansion's fifty-foot wide frontage, and came with an additional thousand square feet of air rights.

Inside Ghislaine's NY mansion

Maxwell began entertaining Park Avenue types there who noted its *Downton Abbey* meets Art Deco vibe, with brightly colored rooms and mirrored surfaces.

'A mix of heavy and heavy,' as one society friend

put it.Maxwell then listed her address at the Companies House register in London as St Thomas, the capital of the US Virgin Islands, where Epstein had a private island, and gave her nationality as American. Her only recorded business interests in Britain are a directorship and shareholding in a make-up company launched by Jemma Kidd, a former model. The company—Jemma Kidd Make-Up— went into liquidation in 2014 with debts of more than $1.7 million.

Meanwhile, it seems that Ghislaine had been discreetly building up a business empire as opaque as her father's. She describes herself as an 'internet operator,' but her office in Manhattan refused to confirm even the name or the nature of her business. It was known that, even though she professed to be of modest means, she had a substantial interest in Magellan, a pioneering internet search engine set up by her elder twin sisters, Isabel and Christine, and sold to ExCite in 1996.

Buckingham Palace found the persistent rumors about her relationship with Prince Andrew wearying. A spokesman said: 'They're good friends and they've known each other for a long time. I believe they were introduced by the Duchess of York.' This referred to the time while Ghislaine was studying and living a high life at Balliol College, Oxford, for three years from 1983.

Like Fergie, she was strong, feisty and loves to party and still known to her friends as 'Good-Time Ghislaine.' However, increasingly, her networking took place out of the public eye. Her antics with Andrew had attracted too much adverse press. The socially prominent women in Ghislaine's 'set' have recently sworn off any kind of publicity. A series of lacerating articles—and the publication of the vapid *Bright Young Things*, written by one of their own, Brooke de Ocampo—portrayed this crowd as a bunch of twits living off their trust funds, the New York *Post* said. Mystery still surrounded where Maxwell's money came from.

Ghislaine and Epstein grouse shooting at Sandringham, the Queen's private estate, at the invitation of Prince Andrew, 2000.

No expense was spared when Prince Andrew threw a surprise birthday party for her at his mother's private estate Sandringham House. It included a weekend shooting party, at a cost of $35,000. Just twenty-five guests rattled around the 273-room Norfolk pile. Epstein's Gulfstream GV-SP carrying the couple landed at RAF Marham, Britain's biggest front-line base and home to four Tornado squadrons. According to the flight log, with them were 'ET'—thought to be Maxwell's assistant Emmy Tayler—and a woman named Kelly Spamm, seemingly a frequent flyer on the Lolita Express.

Sandringham, one of the private estates owned by the Queen of Great Britain

Epstein and Maxwell were also granted a rare honor given to only some foreign dignitaries—a stay at the Royals' much-loved Craigowan lodge, one of

150 buildings on the Balmoral estate in Scotland but one of the few used by the royal family only. This was also the year after the FBI had raided Epstein's Palm Beach mansion where they found evidence of his pedophile interests and a naked image of Ghislaine.

The *Daily Mirror* then weighed in on Prince Andrew, saying 'if ever there was a prize for Royal freeloading Princess Margaret would (obviously) take the top slot, with Prince Andrew coming a close second.'

Margaret was paid £219,000 ($380,000) by the Queen every year to do her public duty, yet she had spent forty years boozing, partying and sleeping with unsuitable men, the paper said. After twenty-two years in the Royal Navy, Andrew was quitting to promote overseas trade and investment for Britain, taking the job from his uncle.

'I suspect this new job is just a cover for the fact he is retiring from the Navy, intends to follow his Auntie Margaret in the ranks of Lazy Goodfornothings, where he will womanize, play golf, yet will still need to justify the fact he's drawing £249,000 [$415,000] from the Civil List—which is where his new job title comes in,' wrote Carole Malone in the *Mirror*. 'As scams go it's not a bad one. But only a Royal could get away with it.'

Before taking up his new duties, Andrew flew

out to Thailand where he was photographed on a luxury yacht in Phuket, surrounded by topless beauties. Ghislaine was also thought to be in Thailand, traveling with Jeffery Epstein. And in March, Virginia Giuffre said she first met Andrew in in London in Maxwell's mews house. The seventeen year old said she had sexual intercourse with the prince, paid for by Epstein, which the prince denies.

The *Sunday People* said that Ghislaine had taken the prince to nightclubs and parties where he'd been pictured looking dazed and confused and sweating heavily.

A Royal source said: 'No-one believes Andrew has tried drugs, but he should look a lot more closely at the sort of people he is hanging around with and where this could all lead. He is moving in a world drenched in hard drugs.

'He is not the most intelligent of men and is easily led. It would be very easy to manipulate him. There is the specter of drugs hanging over almost everyone he's now associating with and almost everywhere he goes and it is really not something a man of his position—and a father of two young daughters—should be getting involved in.

'The Prince is heading for a fall. Somebody needs to shake some sense into him before it's too late.'

Nevertheless in October 2001, on a three-day

visit to New York—the first since the terrorist attack on the World Trade Center, Andrew seized the opportunity to attend a private party thrown for him by Ghislaine Maxwell at her 65th Street townhouse, which was directly opposite Yasser Arafat's New York residence at the Palestine Observer Mission at the UN. As a result the street had to be closed off for the prince. Guests included model Sophie Dahl, socialite Cornelia Guest and a number of attractive young Russian women.

Ghislaine, Naomi Campbell, Donald and Melania Trump, Dolce Gabbano 2002

'He was certainly shown some *glasnost*'—the term used at the time to indicate Soviet Russia's relaxation—said one guest. Andrew had flown out first class at the British taxpayer's expense to represent his mother on a formal visit to Ground Zero. An official from the British Consulate in New York was shocked about the royal antics organized by Ghislaine at her Manhattan mansion: 'This was a complete disgrace. Has this man no sense of decency? He arrives here at this very delicate time representing both Britain and our Queen to pay our respects to the six thousand dead and he goes out partying!'

Indeed, Ghislaine saw no reason to stop partying. In February 2002, she attended a party given by seventy-nine-year-old fashion designer Pierre Cardin at Maxim's de Paris on Madison Avenue. Salman Rushdie and his girlfriend Padma Lakshmi were there. Ghislaine then introduced Bill Clinton to Naomi Campbell who had recently split up with Italian tycoon Flavio Briatore. A society matchmaker, she had also introduced him to Sophie Dahl. Maxwell accompanied Epstein in 2002 when they traveled with President Clinton from New York to London, returning with Naomi Campbell on board two days later. It was another coup for Ghislaine in connecting up Epstein to her increasingly powerful network.

Clinton was then flown around Africa on Epstein's private plane in the company of Chris Tucker and Kevin Spacey, another friend of Ghislaine's. Next, Clinton was then seen having dinner in Manhattan with Maxwell and she was one of the hosts of a fundraiser for his William Jefferson Clinton Library. A $100 donation got you an invitation to the party; $250 got your photo taken with the man himself; while $1,000 got you into the VIP room. Epstein famously gave Clinton and former Israeli Prime Minister Ehud Barak a trip around the world on his own Boeing 727.

Ghislaine and Kevin Spacey, 2002

Spacey got even more royal treatment. That year, he was given a tour of Buckingham Palace given by Prince Andrew while Ghislaine came along. She was photographed lounging on the Queen's throne while Spacey sat on the chair used by the Duke of Edinburgh beside her.

Ghislaine on the throne of the Queen of Great Britain, Kevin Spacey on the throne of Prince Philip, on a private tour of Buckinham Palace by Prince Andrew 2002

'To put this in context, those thrones chairs were used by the Queen and the Duke of Edinburgh in the Coronation,' said former Palace spokesman Dickie Arbiter. 'This is an embarrassment for the Queen. It's a very, very sorry state of affairs.'

Sikh billionaire Vikram Chatwal attended a dinner at Maxwell's house where Prince Andrew was guest of honor. He told a joke about Prince Charles and Camilla Parker Bowles. Ghislaine topped this when she told a story about how she flew a Blackhawk helicopter in Colombia and fired a rocket into a supposed terrorist camp.

'Ghislaine is just the most rocking babe I've ever

met,' said Chatwal. 'She blew up a tank. That is amazing. After that, my perception of her completely changed. I said, "You have to be the coolest person alive."'

She was now so rich and famous that she became a target of criminals. On January 9, 2003, Ghislaine had her maid and butler arrested. They were husband and wife. She noticed that some of her belongings were vanishing from her East 65th Street townhouse.

'She started to realize stuff was missing,' said a detective on the case. He added that the homeowner undertook an investigation, which led her to the basement apartment in her building where her maid and butler lived. Her search revealed some familiar items.

'She found her Christmas gifts there,' the detective said, 'and $7,600 missing from her safe.'

Some of the gifts were actually discovered in the oven. A spokeswoman for the Manhattan District Attorney's office, said that in addition to the cash, $10,000 in clothing and jewelry were also taken. According to the NYPD, when Ms. Maxwell ventured into her staff's quarters in the cellar, she allegedly found more than just her money and her stocking stuffers. She told the police that she saw what the cops described as 'an undetermined amount of credit cards and what appeared to be fraudulent drivers' licenses and license plates.' The couple were arrested pursuant to a search warrant and charged with criminal possession of stolen property and grand larceny.

Knowing first-hand about problems with domestic servants, Maxwell was naturally at the launch of Quintessentially, a new concierge service, at Sotheby's in New York, where Moby, actress Sophie Dahl, Ben Chaplin, TV personality David Frost, and the like were entertained by the Opera Babes. Tom Parker-Bowles was on the board of the company, but his mother Camilla Parker-Bowles, Prince Charles's wife, could not make an appearance as she was forbidden to leave the UK on the brink of the war with Iraq.

Even the palace was taking note of her rising star in the rarified world of royalty. Prince Charles' new private secretary Mark Bolland, brought into raise Camilla's profile, ridiculed Prince Andrew's 'obsession with the airhead-mwahmwah friends of Ghislaine Maxwell.' These presumably included Princess Alexandra of Greece, Lulu de Kwiatowski, Alexander Vreeland, and Amy Fine Collins who turned out for the launched of Ashley Hicks' book about his late father, interior designer David Hicks at the Gucci store on Madison Avenue where British blueblood Rufus Albemarle pretended to help himself to a five-finger, stuffing his pockets with Gucci goodies. He unloaded all the booty before leaving, according to the *Daily News*.

Ghislaine and Luc Brunel on Epstein's Little Saint James island in 2003. Epstein victims accuse Brunel of being a sex trafficker. He was arrested by French police in Paris in 2021 and charged with rape of minors.

Later Ghislaine was seen at the launch of model-hotelier India Hicks' *Island Life*, the coffee table book she produced with photographer David Loftus and her husband, David Flint Wood, about their beloved Harbour Island in the Bahamas, alongside Ralph Lauren, Prince Dmitri and Prince Michel of Yugoslavia, and Princess Alexandra of Greece. Then there was launch of John Varvatos men's fragrance launch at the Canal Room, where Maxwell joined Michael Imperioli, John McDonald, Carson Kressley, Daniela Pestova, Larissa Bond, Patricia Velasquez, Rocco DiSpirito, and Yvonne Scio.

Although Ghislaine had given up her directorship of Oxford United in 1991, she was seen in the boardroom of the Matchroom Stadium, the east London home of Leyton Orient football club in February 2004. Leyton Orient were playing Oxford United and Ghislaine was being entertained in the directors' box. Despite her previous involvement with Oxford United, when her father and brother ran the club, she hadn't been to see them play for years. However, she did retain a small shareholding in the club.

Ghislaine and the Duchess of York, Prince Andrew's ex wife, at the New York launch of jewelry store to billionaires, Asprey's, 2004

When it was mooted that movie about her father called *Citizen Maxwell* was going into production, she said: 'I am sure they will have some sensational twist to my father's murder.' Speaking at a book launch for Elsa Klensch at Thom, she added: 'There is always a different bizarre theory to what happened. I really have no idea myself… One thing I can tell you emphatically is that my father did not commit suicide.' However, she was puzzled by the project. 'It makes me quite wary that no one from the film company has contacted anyone in my family,' she said. The film was never made.

After 2004 Indian Ocean tsunami killed at least 230,000 people, Ghislaine turned up at *Vanity Fair*'s relief auction at the Twentieth Century Theatre in Westbourne Grove alongside Lady Gabriella Windsor and her boyfriend Aatish Taseer. The biggest laugh came at the expense of Ghislaine's old friend. 'His Royal Highness Prince Andrew has kindly donated three trips on his helicopter to the golf course of your choice,' quipped comedian Griff Rhys Jones. It was a joke referring to the many free rides the prince received in his capacity as trade envoy.

By 2005 – when, in March, Florida police first started trash pulls at Epstein's Palm Beach mansion – Ghislaine's celebrity rule seemed unstoppable. Her life in the US was a whirlwind of Hollywood royalty. Back in New York in April 2005, Maxwell was on hand at the Maritime Hotel with Tarita Brando, Helena Christensen and Johnny Pigozzi to celebrate Air Tahiti's first non-stop flight from New York to the island. The hotel's

Hiro ballroom was transformed into a Polynesian paradise with seventy native dancers, tattooed male musicians, Maori choirs, $500,000 of local pearls and the president of French Polynesia, Oscar Temeru. Then there was the launch of Valentino's new fragrance V at The Four Seasons restaurant where she joined the likes of Aby Rosen and Samantha Boardman, Sante D'Orazio, Barbara de Kwiatkowski, Damon Dash and Rachel Roy, Cari Modine, Betsy Bloomingdale, Veronica Hearst, Stephen and Christine Schwarzman and Amy Fine Collins. The DJ was Mark Rosen and many of them continued the fun at Bungalow 8.

Her life was a world-wide merry go round. Maxwell attended the wedding in Barbados of Jemma Kidd, wearing a Christian Lacroix dress, and English aristocrat Arthur Mornington, who was in line to become the Duke of Wellington, in a Ralph Lauren suit. *Vogue* was planning a big fall feature on the tropical nuptials which took place in the ten-acre gardens of the Kidd family home, right next door to the island's renowned Sandy Lane hotel. Guests also included Jemma's younger supermodel sister, Jodie Kidd, Lady Victoria Hervey, Mario Testino and the magazine's editor Anna Wintour. Could anything bring down the woman who, after she seemed down at heel for a few years after the death of her unscrupulous father, was once again a millionaire many times over?

6

IN THE FRAME

Hair line cracks had already appeared in 2002, however. In that year, Maxwell was named in a lawsuit, alongside Epstein and his benefactors Leslie and Abigail Wexner, when artist Nelson Shanks sued for the non-payment of $325,000 for a portrait of the Wexners which they did not like. Epstein was to have made the portrait a gift to the Wexners, while Maxwell had made contact with Shanks about the commission, setting up the deal, according to court documents.

In a 2003 *Vanity Fair* profile of him following the unwanted attention, Epstein told journalist Vicky Ward that Maxwell was 'his best friend' but was not on his payroll, although she often acted as his fixer. Court files referred to her as his 'actual or apparent agent'. The secretive duo were described as 'residents of the US Virgin Islands', where Epstein owned a seventy-acre island hideaway.

'Nelson made many overtures to the Wexners and Maxwell to view the work and comment, and they never took him up,' said Jeffrey Hofferman, the artist's lawyer. It was as part of this profile that Ward spoke for the first time to Maria Farmer who told her how she had been sexually abused by Epstein and Maxwell on a trip to Zorro Ranch with Maxwell and Epstein. Her sixteen year old sister had been abused by Epstein on Little Saint James island. Under pressure, *Vanity Fair* never published this part of her research.

Sisters: sixteen-year-old Annie and artist Maria Farmer in 1996

It took until August 2006 for the next crack to appear when the *Palm Beach Post* reported that the police were taking an interest at the goings on at

140

Epstein's waterfront mansion on El Brillo Way where he lived in Palm Beach luxury. Three black Mercedes sat in his garage, alongside a green Harley-Davidson. His jet waited at a hangar at Palm Beach International Airport. At home, a private chef and a small staff stood at the ready. From a window in his mansion, he could look out on the Intracoastal Waterway and the Florida skyline.

Although he made no effort to be part of the Palm Beach social scene, Epstein made his presence felt. Among his charitable donations were $100,000 he gave to the Ballet Foria and $90,000 to the Palm Beach Police Department. He seemed to be a man who had everything—including a best girlfriend and fixer who was the doyenne of New York society and the global jetset.

In March 2005, a worried mother had contacted Palm Beach police. She said another parent had overheard a conversation between their children and was afraid her fourteen-year-old daughter had been molested by a man on the island. Detectives interviewed the girl, who told them a friend had invited her to a rich man's house to perform a massage. She said the friend told her to say she was eighteen if asked. At the house, she said she was paid $300 after stripping to her panties and massaging the man while he masturbated.

The investigation took off after the girl identified the man who had paid her as Epstein from a photograph. Police arranged for garbage trucks to set aside trash from the house so police could sift through it. They set up a video camera to record the comings and goings, and they monitored an airport hangar and his private jet's arrivals and departures.

They learnt that the friend who had taken the fourteen-year-old to Epstein's house was Haley Robertson, a student at Palm Beach Community College. In a sworn statement at police headquarters, Robson, then eighteen, admitted she had taken at least six girls to visit Epstein, all between the ages of fourteen and sixteen. Epstein paid her for each visit, she said. During the drive back to her house, she told detectives, 'I'm like a Heidi Fleiss'—then a famous celebrity madam in Hollywood.

Police interviewed five alleged victims and seventeen other witnesses. Their report shows some of the girls said they had been instructed to have sex with another woman in front of Epstein, and one said she had direct intercourse with him. As well as living with Epstein at least part-time in New York, Maxwell also stayed at his Palm Beach house.

'Ms. Maxwell was like the lady of the house,' said Alfredo Rodriguez, who worked in the Palm Beach mansion in 2005, explaining that household expenses were paid out of a bank account in Ghislaine's name, according to a deposition in a later court case.

In October, police searched the Palm Beach mansion. They discovered photos of naked, young-looking females, just as several of the girls had described in interviews. Similar pictures were found stashed in an armoire and on the computers seized at the house (although police found only bare cables where other computers had been). Some bathrooms were stocked with soap in the shape of sex organs, and various sex toys, such as a 'twin torpedo' vibrator and creams and lubricants available at erotic specialty shops, were stowed near the massage tables set up in several rooms upstairs.

A naked portrait of Ghislaine in Epstein's Florida home

Hidden cameras were found in the garage area and inside a clock on Epstein's desk, alongside a girl's high school homework. Two of Epstein's former employees told detectives that young-looking girls showed up to perform massages on Epstein two or three times a day when he was in town. Unbeknownst to the Florida police, this was very similar to the 1996 FBI and NYPD complaint made about Epstein by the sixteen-year-old Annie Farmer who had gone to New Mexico and said that Maxwell had taught her the basics of giving a massage.

The Florida girls were well rewarded. A chef cooked for them. Other employees gave them rides and handed out hundreds of dollars at a time. Rodriguez told detectives he was told to send a dozen roses to one teenage girl after a high school drama performance. Others were given rental cars. One received a $200 Christmas bonus, according to the police. Rodriguez also said in sworn testimony he was terrified of Maxwell.

However, other forces were at work. One girl interviewed in Orlando told the police that a private investigator had asked her the same questions. Epstein's former employees told them the same thing. There were complaints that some private eyes were posing as police officers. Epstein's local attorney, Guy Fronstin, said that the investigators worked for Roy

Black, a high-powered Miami lawyer who had defended the likes of Kennedy scion William Kennedy Smith and TV host Rush Limbaugh. It seemed that the private eyes were conducting a parallel investigation.

Harvard law professor Alan Dershowitz arrived in Palm Beach with information obtained from the website MySpace.com where they discussed their use of alcohol and marijuana. Others had criminal records or troubled backgrounds that cast doubt on the teenagers' reliability. At least one of them, Epstein's legal team said, lied when she told police she was younger than eighteen when she started performing massages for Epstein. Although two of the victims and their families claimed they had been harassed or threatened, Epstein's lawyers maintained their private investigators did nothing illegal or unethical during their enquiries.

Soon relations between police and prosecutors began to unravel. At a key meeting with prosecutors and the defense, the lead investigator Detective Joseph Recarey did not show up according to Epstein's attorney Jack Goldberger.

Later in April, Recarey learnt the state attorney's office had offered Epstein a plea deal that would not require him to serve jail time or receive a felony conviction. He protested. On May 1, the police asked prosecutors to approve warrants to arrest Epstein on four counts of unlawful sexual activity with a minor and to charge his personal assistant, Sarah Kellen, then twenty-seven, for allegedly arranging the visits. Police officers also wanted to charge Haley Robson.

On the same day the warrants were requested, Palm Beach Police Chief Michael Reiter wrote to State Attorney Barry Krischer asking he disqualify himself from the case if he would not act. Two weeks later, prosecutors decided to take the case to a grand jury.

Their indictment was handed down in July. But instead of being slapped with a charge of unlawful sexual activity with a minor, Epstein was charged with one count of felony solicitation of prostitution, which carries a maximum penalty of five years in prison. He was booked into the Palm Beach County Jail on July 23 and released hours later.

Epstein's legal team said they did not dispute that he had girls over for massages, but their claims that they had sexual encounters with him lack credibility.

'They are incapable of being believed,' said Goldberger. 'They had criminal records. They had accusations of theft made against them by their employers. There was evidence of drug use by some of them.'

The Palm Beach Police Department returned Epstein's $90,000 donation and asked the FBI to investigate the case.

Meanwhile, back in New York, Ghislaine continued as before and had introduced Prince Andrew to American actress and *Playboy* model Angie Everhart. She spent time at Royal Lodge, Andrew's newly renovated home in Windsor Great Park, following her surprise appearance at his daughter Beatrice's eighteenth birthday party in 2006.

Harvey Weinstein, Epstein and Ghislaine at Princess Beatrice's fancy-dress eighteenth birthday party at the Queen's Windsor Castle, invited by Prince Andrew

As mentioned, also on the guest list were Maxwell and Epstein, a month after he had been charged with solicitation. Andrew said that wasn't aware at the time the invitation was sent out 'what was going on in the United States' and Epstein never mentioned it. However, Maxwell would certainly have known as

Epstein's best girlfriend and fixer. Harvey Weinstein was also a guest of the prince's.

That September Andrew and Ghislaine were at a dinner hosted by celebrity psychiatrist Samantha Boardman at Lever House. For the two of them, it was business as usual despite the sex investigation of their friend.

Next Ghislaine was seen at a gala hosted by Google co-founder Larry Page at Google HQ in Mountain View, California, raising $2 million for the X Prize Foundation. Other guests included Sir Richard Branson, Tipper Gore, Jerry Brown, Arianna Huffington, and the tech billionaire Elon Musk. Then it was on to Chinatown Brasserie to celebrate the twenty-fifth anniversary of Nicole Miller's debut in the fashion industry with the likes of author Jay McInerney and scion Anne Hearst, Tama Janowitz, Robert Pittman, Michelle Hicks, Jason Binn, and celebrity restaurateur André Balazs.

The unravelling gathered pace in October 2007, however. According to the *Miami Herald*, US Attorney Alexander Acosta, later Donald Trump's US Secretary of Labor, had a secret meeting with one of Epstein's attorneys over breakfast in the Marriott in West Palm Beach. They agreed that Epstein would plead guilty to minor felony state charges of procuring a person under eighteen for prostitution and register as a sex offender.

In return, Epstein and any possible co-conspirators would be immune to any further charges. This would mean that Epstein would only serve just under thirteen months in prison then ten months on probation. The deal, which was brokered without the knowledge of Epstein's victims, meant that four women subsequently named as Epstein's alleged accomplices—Nadia Marcinkova, who would later be described as his 'Yugoslavian sex slave' and the 'live-in lesbian,' Sarah Kellen, Adriana Ross and Lesley Groff—were not charged.

Ghislaine Maxwell was not named in the indictment. However, her name was written on retrieved message pads, flight manifests and other documents found by the police in Epstein's home. Handwritten call logs named Maxwell and contained messages saying: 'She is wondering if 2:30 ok cuz she needs to stay in school,' 'She has females for Mr JE,' and 'I have a female for him.'

The excuse for this sweetheart deal, Epstein's lawyers insisted, was that he had been unaware of the girls' ages. Epstein told the *New York Times* that he had replaced them with a full-time male masseur and, when he went to jail in Miami, he set his email to auto-reply that he was 'on vacation.' No further investigations were made in New York, New Mexico, or the

Virgin Islands. The case was contained to south Florida, some said because of Epstein's secret service connections and incriminating evidence on powerful people.

On June 30, 2008, Epstein pleaded guilty to 'felony, solicitation of prostitution and procuring a person under the age of 18 for prostitution' in two counts respectively. In doing so, he escaped charges, including statutory rape, that could have resulted in a life sentence. In return for Epstein pleading guilty to the lesser charge, he was sentenced to eighteen months in jail and house arrest for a year. He would also be registered as a sex offender for the remainder of his life.

However, instead of being sent to a federal penitentiary, Epstein was given a private wing at the Palm Beach County Stockade Facility and had his own personal security guards. He paid $128,000 to the Palm Beach County Sheriff's Department for the privilege. The cell door was left open and he was given 'liberal access' to a room with a television. It was argued that these arrangements were made for Epstein because he may otherwise have been victimized by other inmates.

After just three months, he was granted work release that allowed him out of jail for up to sixteen hours, seven days a week at an office at the 'Florida Science Foundation', an organization he had set up.

He could also spend two of those hours at his Palm Beach home where he had committed the original offences, later being confined there under house arrest.

While Epstein was out of the picture, Ghislaine was reported to be house hunting and attending the usual round of celebrity parties. She was seen with Prince Andrew at the Monkey Bar in New York. The couple talked animatedly for some time.

But the cat was out of the bag. Without Ghislaine knowing it yet, her jetset life was to come crashing down. One of Epstein's alleged victims, identified only as Jane Doe, sued Epstein for $30 million. She claimed that in 2005, when she was just fifteen, she was lured to his home in Palm Beach when he offered her $200 for a massage. As soon as they were in a bedroom together, he demanded she remove her clothes and sexually assaulted her, according to a lawsuit filed in a federal court in West Palm Beach on January 24, 2008. She said he touched himself and her while she was naked from the waist up, and was lured back to the mansion on at least one other occasion. Lily Ann Sanchez, Mr Epstein's lawyer, said the girl's allegations were false and motivated by money. The case was quickly settled out of court.

In July another federal lawsuit was filed against Epstein. This time, the 'Jane Doe' claimed that

Ghislaine Maxwell had recruited her from Donald Trump's Mar-a-Lago Club when she was just sixteen. At Mar-a-Lago, Trump insisted on a three to two female to male ratio and knew Epstein well. 'He always saw Epstein around younger girls, but to his knowledge, none were underage', he claimed to the girl's lawyer—he later banned Epstein from the club after he made contact with the underage daughter of one of the club's members. She worked there as a changing-room assistant for $9 an hour. The lawsuit said Maxwell told the girl, and her father who was an employee at the club, that she could learn massage therapy and earn a 'great deal of money.'

The girl told the *Daily Mail*: 'I was wearing my uniform—a white miniskirt and a skin-tight white polo top—and studying an anatomy book when I was approached by this striking woman in her mid-40s with a very proper British accent: Ghislaine. I told her I wanted to become a masseuse and she said she worked for a very wealthy gentleman who was looking for a traveling masseuse. I'd get training and be paid well.'

The Jane Doe in this suit was Virginia Roberts, later Giuffre. In a lawsuit Roberts filed against Epstein in 2009, she said Maxwell took her to Epstein's home and into a massage room, where he was lying naked on a table. 'Ms. Maxwell then took off her own shirt and left on her underwear and started rubbing her breasts against (Epstein's) body... showing plaintiff what she was expected to do,' the suit says. Maxwell then told her to take off her clothes and 'straddle' Epstein.

'The encounter escalated, with defendant and Ms. Maxwell sexually assaulting, battering and abusing plaintiff in various ways and in various locations,' the suit said. Afterwards, Maxwell and Epstein told her to come back the next day. They got her to quit her job and become a full-time 'masseuse,' the suit said, giving Epstein multiple 'massages' per day at his various estates around the world.

'Often, plaintiff was joined by Ms. Maxwell, Ms. Maxwell's assistant, and/or a countless array of young women who would be brought to one of the defendant's homes,' the suit said.

However, the alleged victim said that she was not only required to satisfy Epstein's 'every sexual whim,' but that she also was exploited by Epstein's adult male peers. They included royalty, politicians, academicians, businessmen and others in various locations around the world, the suit said.

On the other hand, Roberts said of Epstein: 'I felt that he and Ghislaine really cared for me. We'd do family things, like watch *Sex And The City* and eat popcorn.'

While Maxwell was abroad, Roberts said, she was tasked by Epstein with a number of daily chores including 'massages, sex, and even dressing' him, but also to recruit more girls to fulfill his sick sexual lust. Virginia said in her diary: 'I would offer [girls] money to come meet my gentlemen friend and tell them I'd show them how to massage.'

Maxwell agreed to sit for a deposition in a related civil case in 2009, but then backed out at the last minute, court papers said. Maxwell said her mom was sick and she was leaving the country for the UK with no plans to return.

Ghislaine at Chelsea Clinton's wedding in July 2010

'Yet a short time later, Maxwell was photographed at Chelsea Clinton's July 2010 wedding in Rhinebeck,

New York, confirming the suspicion that she was indeed still in the country and willing to say anything to avoid her deposition,' Roberts said in papers filed in Florida federal court. Curiously, in the same month, 116E 65th St was put up for sale for the first time for $10 million, though no sale went through in the end.

The Chelsea Clinton connection was yet another social triumph for multimillionaire Maxwell. She became close to the her in 2009 when she vacationed on a yacht with Chelsea with whom she got along brilliantly. By this time, her name had already been publicly linked to the Epstein scandal. She was at that time romantically linked to billionaire Ted Waitt, the founder of Gateway. In 2013, Ghislaine was still part of the Clintons' orbit when she participated in the Clinton Global Initiative in 2013.

'It wasn't until 2015 that Chelsea and Marc became aware of the horrific allegations against Ghislaine Maxwell', their spokesperson claimed, 'Chelsea and Marc were friendly with her because of her relationship with a dear friend of theirs. When that relationship ended, Chelsea and Marc's friendship with her ended as well.'

Epstein himself did sit for a deposition, but repeatedly pleaded the fifth. Representatives for Prince Andrew and Maxwell have consistently denied wrongdoing.

A dozen other lawsuits against the billionaire money manager said his modus operandi in the initial visit was the same. The minor was taken to Epstein's mansion on El Brillo Way and led upstairs by one of Epstein's assistants to a spa room where he would ask the girl to perform massages or various sex acts, which he would pay her for.

The lawsuit also said that Epstein took the girl to New York City, Santa Fe, Los Angeles, San Francisco, St. Louis, Europe, the Caribbean, and Africa. In all of these locations, she was required to engage in sex acts with him and other women, including other underage girls.

'Most of these acts of abuse occurred during a time when the defendant knew that the plaintiff was approximately fifteen, sixteen and seventeen years old and, after years of daily sexual exploitation continued into her adulthood… until she fled at age nineteen,' the lawsuit said. It also alleged that when Epstein and Maxwell celebrated the girl's sixteenth birthday, Epstein joked that he would have to trade her in because she was getting too old for him.

Epstein's 'predilection for young girls was well known to those who regularly procured them for him and to his circle of friends,' the lawsuit said. Epstein was said to display photos of naked underage girls throughout his homes in Palm Beach, New York City,

Santa Fe, and the U.S. Virgin Islands. The alleged victim said she saw a nude picture of herself displayed in Epstein's Palm Beach home. She believed that the nude photos of her as a minor were confiscated by the Palm Beach County Sheriff's Office during the October 2005 execution of a search warrant on his Palm Beach home and were still in the custody of law enforcement. This case was also settled. U.S. District Judge Kenneth A. Marra then dismissed both complaints 'with prejudice,' meaning they could not be refiled.

Epstein settled more than a dozen lawsuits brought by underage girls. Seven victims reached a last-minute deal last week, days before a scheduled trial. Each received well over $1 million—an amount that would hardly dent Epstein's $2 billion net worth.

While under house arrest, Epstein—a keen car collector—put his most prized vehicle, a 2003 Ferrari 575M Maranello, on sale for $159,000. To conceal the car's origins, he transferred the title of the car to his pilot. The named vendor of the Ferrari is listed as one Larry Visoski, who identified himself in Federal Election Commission filings in the past as the chief pilot of Air Ghislane Inc, owned by Epstein, presumably a corporate reference to Ghislaine Maxwell.

Meanwhile, she remained the toast of Manhattan society and was still doing the rounds in New York. In

May 2009, she was seen at the book launch of *Rogues'*
Gallery, subtitled *The Secret Story of the Lust, Lies, Greed,*
and Betrayals that Made The Metropolitan Museum of Art.
She also attended the annual Alzheimer's Association's
New York Rita Hayworth Gala, traditionally one of
New York City's most prestigious, glamorous, and
successful philanthropic events. Held in the Waldorf's
Grand Ballroom it raised $1.5 million.

Calvin Klein (standing), billionaire Aby Rosen and Ghislaine, 2009

Then in December, Prince Andrew mingled with
the city's most glamorous including Laura Brown,
Mary Alice Stephenson, Tatiana von Furstenberg and
a bevy of models at a party at the Ghislaine Maxwell's
townhouse. 'Since Ghislaine recently split up with her
partner, this was almost like a singles party. The prince

seemed to be enchanted with many of the women in the room, especially one particular willowy blonde,' the New York *Post* said.

Then on February 20, 2011, the *News of the World* published a picture of Prince Andrew and Epstein taking a stroll in Central Park, under the headline: 'Prince Andy & The Paedo—Royal's Dodgy Pal Exclusive.' The newspaper revealed that Andrew stayed for four days with Epstein at his New York townhouse, the previous December, shortly after he had completed his sentence. He had also been guest of honor at a dinner celebrating Epstein's release. Other guests included Woody Allen, TV anchors Katie Couric and George Stephanopoulos, comedienne Chelsea Handler.

'It is understood Andrew—fourth in line to the throne and a UK trade ambassador—was there on a private visit, not official business. But his continued contact with shamed Epstein, who is reportedly worth $2 billion, will once again call his judgement into question,' the newspaper said.

It also reported that one of Epstein's alleged victims was a fifteen-year-old who had been taken to Epstein's home by a friend.

'He jumped in the shower and told me to remove my clothes down to my bra and panties. We were both like, 'What are we going to do now?"' she said. Epstein then stripped naked. 'He basically was touching himself and touching my friend and trying to touch me.'

They were each paid $200 before being sent home in a taxi. 'I felt disgusting. I felt violated,' she said. Epstein made an out-of-court settlement with her.

The newspaper also mentioned that Andrew had been introduced to Epstein by Ghislaine Maxwell. A week later Virginia Roberts—now Giuffre—in a bombshell article dropped her anonymity and told a newspaper that she was the fifteen-year-old who had been seduced by Epstein.

'Basically, I was training to be a prostitute for him and his friends who shared his interest in young girls,' she said fearlessly under her own name.

Giuffre was taking an enormous risk by going public against these rich, powerful and well-connected people. They could afford the best lawyers and make her life a misery, even though she lived in Australia. From this moment on, the story became a modern version of David and Goliath with Virginia ceaselessly taking on Epstein, and vanquishing the billionaire again and again, despite the uneven odds. She did it by candidly telling her story.

'Ghislaine sent me to a dentist to have my teeth whitened and I went for Brazilian waxes. He wanted me to look pre-pubescent.'

Virginia Roberts Giuffre when she bravely dropped her anonyimity in 2011 and fought billion-aire Epstein under her own name rather than as a Jane Doe.

Maxwell, would encourage the girls to get all dolled up in slinky costumes, she said. But other times it was Epstein who requested them to wear racy getups.

'Ghislaine would take me to dress up to surprise J.E., or Jeffrey would ask me to get dressed up,' Roberts told her lawyers.

'That would include wearing a tiny little skirt with

nothing underneath, a white-collared shirt that you would be wearing to school with a tie in it, tied up in a bow, my hair in pigtails, stockings on up to my knees, and I would go in there and act like a kid and we'd do role playing.' Maxwell would also supply them with latex outfits the money manager loved, she said.

'After about two years… he said, 'I've got a good friend, and I need you to fly to the island to entertain him, massage him and make him feel how you make me feel,' she told the *Mail*. 'He didn't spell out what I had to do—he didn't have to. He'd trained me to do whatever a man wanted.'

She said she had decided to come forward with her story after seeing photos published last week showing Epstein strolling with Prince Andrew in Central Park. She had met the prince three times during her four-year stint with Epstein. The first time they met, she was seventeen.

The FBI had contacted her after finding pictures of her while investigating Epstein. She was then living in Australia.

The *Mail* also printed the now famous photograph showing a smiling Andrew with his arm around Roberts' waist. The photo was taken at the London home of Ghislaine Maxwell when she visited London in 2001, Giuffre said. Maxwell told her: 'You've got a big day. We've gotta go shopping. You need a dress because you're going to dance with a prince tonight.' Maxwell bought her a designer frock, a $9,000 Burberry bag, perfume, and make-up.

Later that day the prince arrived at Maxwell's house, Giuffre said, with his police protection officers, and she was introduced to him. Ghislaine asked Andrew how old he thought she was.

'He guessed seventeen, and they all laughed,' Giuffre said. 'Ghislaine made a joke that I was getting too old for Jeffrey. She said: 'He'll soon have to trade her in.''

The four went out to dinner, Roberts sitting between Epstein and the prince.

'Andrew was making eye contact with me at every chance and concentrating on my plunging V-neck top,' she told the *Mail on Sunday*. 'He didn't ask me anything about myself. I just sat there with a smile frozen on my lips. Ghislaine had whispered: 'The prince seems really interested in you.''

Next was one of London's most exclusive night-clubs.

'We went on to [Andrew's favourite night club] Tramp. We were led into a VIP area and Andrew got me a cocktail from the bar then he asked me to dance. He was the most hideous dancer I had ever seen. He was grabbing my hips and he was pouring with perspiration and he had this cheesy smile. I was used to being used for sex by men but it was not behavior that I was used to in public, and not from a prince who had daughters. I felt everyone was watching us.'

It was plain the way the evening was going to turn out.

'After about an hour-and-a-half we drove back to Ghislaine's,' said Giuffre. 'All of us went upstairs and I asked Jeffrey to snap a picture of me with the Prince. I wanted something to show my Mom. Ghislaine and Jeffrey left us after that, and later Andrew left. In the morning Ghislaine said, 'You did well. He had fun.' We flew straight back to the States. I suspected that the only reason we went to London was that I was a 'gift' to Andrew. It was made clear to me that my job was to do whatever pleased him.'

The trip also included stops in Paris, Granada, and Tangier. Giuffre said Epstein paid her $15,000.

In December 2009, Giuffre had first filed a lawsuit against Epstein as Jane Doe 102. She was one of nearly two dozen women who settled lawsuits against Epstein for undisclosed amounts, all alleging they were sexually abused by him as minors. Giuffre also told the *Mail* that Epstein and Maxwell said they wanted her to have their child.

That was her 'wake-up call' to get out of the situation. While Giuffre's revelations put Maxwell's name all over the papers, it was Prince Andrew they were still only gunning for. The London *Daily Telegraph* said: 'The fact that Epstein is a convicted sex offender with an industrial-scale appetite for young girls appeared not to offend the Duke, who has been only too ready to accept his hospitality. Even to the extent of accepting massages at Epstein's home in Palm Beach, Florida, scene of lurid happenings involving girls recruited locally to serve as 'erotic masseurs."

Further down the story, the newspaper drew attention to Maxwell's involvement, saying: 'A onetime partner of Epstein, she remained close to him after their parting and, according to witnesses, played a key role in organizing, and sometimes participating in, his secret sexual life.'

It again mentioned that Roberts had been recruited by Maxwell to have sex with Epstein and 'described being flown to various locations to service the needs of men of widely differing ages... Her encounter with Andrew occurred in early 2001. After dinner in London with Epstein and Miss Maxwell, she and the Duke were said to have been left alone.'

Roberts claimed to have had a second sexual encounter with Andrew at Epstein's New York home. Maxwell told her to take the prince upstairs for a massage. 'I took him upstairs to the Dungeon. He undressed and lay face down on the table. I started with his feet, then his calves the way Jeffrey liked it.'

She said she had sex with the prince on the massage table, but received no extra payment, 'just my usual hourly rate, which at that time was $200.'

Roberts said that she had also met Bill Clinton during her stay with Epstein, though she had never been 'lent out' to him.

'I'd have been about seventeen at the time I flew to the Caribbean with Jeffrey and then Ghislaine Maxwell went to pick up Bill in a huge black helicopter that Jeffrey had bought her,' she told the *Daily Mail*. 'We all dined together that night. Jeffrey was at the head of the table. Bill was at his left. I sat across from him. Emmy Tayler, Ghislaine's blonde British assistant, sat at my right.

'Ghislaine was at Bill's left and at the left of Ghislaine there were two olive-skinned brunettes who'd flown in with us from New York. I'd never met them before. I'd say they were no older than seventeen, very innocent-looking.

'They weren't there for me. They weren't there for Jeffrey or Ghislaine because I was there to have sex with Jeffrey on the trip. Maybe Jeffrey thought they would entertain Bill, but I saw no evidence that he was interested in them. He and Jeffrey and Ghislaine seemed to have a very good relationship. Bill was very funny.'

'After dinner I gave Jeffrey an erotic massage. I

don't remember seeing Bill again on the trip but I assume Ghislaine flew him back.'

On another occasion Roberts said she was involved in an orgy on the island with Epstein, Prince Andrew and 'seven Russian girls who didn't speak a word of English' who arrived with a modeling agent. The girls were told to pose topless in provocative positions for photographs, 'then we were told to assemble in a big cabana. When I walked in, Andrew and Jeffrey were seated in chairs. Jeffrey directed us with hand gestures to start undressing and then we were instructed to start kissing and touching each other. Jeffrey and the prince were laughing and then I stripped and I performed a sex act on Andrew. There was a dinner the next day and then Andrew was gone.'

Giuffre said that Ghislaine had told her that she'd hit hard times when Jeffrey offered her a job. Then, because of her ability to procure girls, she became a vital asset to him.

More information about what happened on the island was provided by a South African couple named Cathy and Miles Alexander were hired to manage the property on Epstein's private island Little St James in 1999 after being interviewed by Ghislaine Maxwell and one of Epstein's lawyers. After apparently passing the interview, they were invited to meet Epstein in New York.

'It was very strange,' said Miles. 'We were taken by a driver to an office near Madison Square Garden. A gentleman wearing a polo shirt and jeans stepped out of the lift, asked if we had a good trip, shook our hands and left. That was it. Then Miss Maxwell came back and said we had the job.'

They recalled being troubled by the sight of teenaged girls arriving and walking around the house naked.

'I saw some girls who I thought were very young looking—about sixteen or seventeen easily—and it bugged me because I have a daughter... I didn't like the idea that another woman's child was in that situation,' Cathy Alexander said. 'They looked like they had stepped out of an underwear catalogue. They walked around with very few clothes on or lounged around by the pool with nothing on.'

When they returned to New York, Ghislaine explained more of their duties.

'She said we had to keep quiet about what we saw or heard on the island,' Cathy recalled. 'She told us that although Mr Epstein and she were a couple, we would see lots of beautiful girls passing in and out, but that was his nature.

'She said that he gets what he wants but that she was always the 'Queen Bee' and the one in charge. She often described herself in this way. Although she could be very friendly, I discovered that she was also rather arrogant.'

Other damning evidence against Prince Andrew and Ghislaine Maxwell surfaced.

Giving evidence in a video deposition, Juan Alessi, Epstein's maintenance man in Palm Beach from 1991 until 2002, said the duke visited the house four or five times a year, enjoying daily massages during his stays. The pool area was decorated with pictures of naked women.

Describing a constantly changing cast of characters, including European models, Mr Alessi observed: 'Miss Maxwell was the one that recruits. I remember one occasion or two occasions she would say to me: 'Juan, give me a list of all the spas in Palm Beach County.' And I will drive her from one to the other one. And she will go in, drop business cards, and she come out. She will recruit the girls.'

The place was run 'like a hotel,' he said, recalling that Prince Andrew stayed in the 'blue' guest room. He remembered pool parties.

'European girls particularly, they were always taking their clothes off,' he said, according to reports. 'I'd have to tell them, 'Look, go away, put something on and then come back here.' ' He said the duke made his own bed and 'was the only guy who left us a tip—and a key chain from the royal palace as a souvenir'.

7

DECLINE AND FALL

While Epstein had served his 2008 sentence and made financial settlements with his victims, it was clear that this would not be the end of the matter. Lawyers for his victims were appalled at the leniency of his punishment. One said: 'The deal stinks to high heaven but the mechanics of how it was arrived at, we're still looking at.'

Ghislaine Maxwell's involvement also invited further scrutiny. In a lawsuit filed in a Federal District Court a victim identified as 'MJ' alleged Epstein was the boss of a 'criminal enterprise' involving sex trafficking of young girls. Sarah Kellen, Nadia Marcinkova, and Ghislaine Maxwell were named as co-conspirators. The document says: 'Maxwell personally brought underage girls to Epstein for him to sexually abuse. Maxwell was also a participant in sexually abusing minor females.' When questioned, Sarah Kellen and Nadia Marcinkova invoked their Fifth

Amendment right against self-incrimination.

Another of Epstein's victims Johanna Sjoberg, who claimed that Andrew put his hand on her breasts while she was sitting on his lap for a photograph, said Maxwell was 'present and joined in the joke, when the girls were invited to sit on Andrew's lap.'

The joke was that they had a latex puppet of Prince Andrew from the satirical TV show *Spitting Image*.

'Ghislaine put the puppet's hand on Virginia's breast, then Andrew put his hand on mine,' Sjoberg said. It was a great joke.' She added, 'Ghislaine made a lot of sexual jokes.'

In a familiar refrain, Sjoberg also said that she had been brought to Epstein's Palm Beach mansion as a masseuse by Maxwell in February 2001.

'Ghislaine asked if I would like to earn $20 an hour doing odd jobs around the house for Epstein,' said Johanna. 'It was mostly to be small errands and that was good money. The first time I met him he was just wearing a small towel. I thought that was odd, but that was how rich people behaved.' Then Ghislaine asked her 'Do you want to make $100 rubbing feet?' Gradually Epstein's demands became sexual. She last saw Maxwell in January 2006.

Other witness statements also alleged that it was Maxwell who recruited the young girls on Epstein's staff, and even kept albums of photographs she took of topless girls at the house. She was said to have had regular massages herself and to have kept sex toys in her room.

On May 10, 2011, Maxwell issued a statement, denying all the allegations against her that had appeared in the media. Letters sent by her lawyers asking for them to be withdrawn had been ignored, her statement said, and Maxwell said she was taking legal action against the newspapers.

'I understand newspapers need stories to sell copies. It is well known that certain newspapers live by the adage, 'why let the truth get in the way of a good story.' However, the allegations made against me are abhorrent and entirely untrue and I ask that they stop,' she said. 'A number of newspapers have shown a complete lack of accuracy in their reporting of this story and a failure to carry out the most elementary investigation or any real due diligence. I am now taking action to clear my name.'

In the wake of the allegations, other members of the Maxwell family kept their heads down. Isabel Maxwell said: 'I make it a rule not to participate in this type of general Maxwell family catch up.'

After consulting her husband Kevin, the normally garrulous Pandora Maxwell—who famously appeared at a window of her Chelsea home in 1992 to shout 'p*** off or I'll call the police,' only to discover that her unwelcome early–morning callers were members of the constabulary who had come to arrest her husband Kevin—said: 'I always put my foot in it and I have to think about the effect on my children.' She has seven of them.

Friends in New York also closed ranks behind Ghislaine, initially. 'No one in café society gives a damn that a fifteen-year-old girl gives massages,' said one frequent charity-benefit guest. 'She gets people into parties and runs around for a lot of people.' As to the fallout from her association with Epstein, he said: 'If you're Mike Huckabee it would matter but not if you're Ghislaine Maxwell.'

British headlines that screamed 'The Prince and the Perv', detailing Andrew's relationship with Epstein and Maxwell, seemed to have sunk in the mid-Atlantic. 'A jail sentence doesn't matter anymore,' said David Patrick Columbia, founder of *New York Social Diary*. 'The only thing that gets you shunned in New York society is poverty.'

And Epstein was anything but poor. Behind closed doors, top publicist Peggy Siegal told the *Daily Beast*: 'I and many others that know him describe him as brilliant. His unique mind is what attracts the world's smartest people to his home.'

With Siegal's help, Epstein hosted a Break Fast

after Yom Kippur. A group of 120 friends brought their children over for a buffet dinner. A New York real-estate heir Jonathan Farkas, who had known Epstein for thirty-five years and visited him while he was in prison, said: 'The side I've been reading about is a side I don't know. Unless I've seen it, I don't focus on it.'

'From a cerebral and business side he's worshipped,' says socialite Debbie Bancroft. 'He's incredibly charming and handsome. He's an extraordinary package so I can see why people don't want to believe what they hear. If people come out of jail and are still successful, people are very forgiving, shockingly so.'

Professor Lawrence Krauss, a theoretical physicist and author of *Quantum Man* who planned scientific conferences with Epstein on St. Thomas and remained close with him throughout his incarceration, said: 'If anything, the unfortunate period he suffered has caused him to really think about what he wants to do with his money and his time, and support knowledge. Jeffrey has surrounded himself with beautiful women and young women but they're not as young as the ones that were claimed.

'As a scientist I always judge things on empirical evidence and he always has women ages nineteen to twenty-three around him, but I've never seen anything else, so as a scientist, my presumption is that whatever the problems were I would believe him over other people.'

Though colleagues criticized him over his relationship with Epstein, Krauss insisted at the time: 'I don't feel tarnished in any way by my relationship with Jeffrey; I feel raised by it.'

While excuses were made for Epstein, Maxwell remained in the clear and continued her globe-trotting ways.

'The last time I saw Ghislaine,' said Vassi Chamberlain, 'was on holiday in 2012. I heard her name shouting from across the street.'

'What are you doing tonight?' she asked. 'Come to dinner on *Akula*.'

This was a two-hundred-foot yacht belonging to Jonathan Faiman, the co-founder of Britain's largest grocery retailer Ocado, and his wife Kira that Ghislaine was staying on.

'There was a mildly uncomfortable atmosphere all evening: She had invited her friends, but the hosts knew none of us,' said Chamberlain. 'It was typical Ghislaine.'

That night Ghislaine talked about her pet project, TerraMar, a non-profit environmental organization she founded at the Blue Ocean Film Festival and Conservation Conference in Monterey, California in 2012. The idea was to create a 'global ocean community' based on the sixty-four percent of the high seas that do not fall under any national jurisdiction.

Ghislaine speaking at the United Nations

Maxwell also spoke at the United Nations and attended meetings there as the founder of the TerraMar Project. She attended the Arctic Circle Assembly in Reykjavik Iceland in 2013 with her future husband Scott Borgerson, who was listed on TerraMar's board of directors. In June 2014, Maxwell and Borgerson spoke at an event in Washington, DC, sponsored by the Council on Foreign Relations, called 'Governing the Ocean Commons: Growing Challenges, New Approaches'. That year, Maxwell also gave a lecture at the University of Texas at Dallas and later, gave a TED talk, about the importance of ocean conservation.

The project aimed to turn the oceans into an online country known as TerraMar. There was a website where you could sign up to become a citizen. Your name would be appended to an area of ocean or you become an ambassador for one of the myriad marine species.

'All citizens of the world are citizens of TerraMar, or citizens of the high seas, if you will, part of the global commons,' said Maxwell. 'But say that you feel a sense of identity, we're giving you passports to it. So, when you go to the site, it's where you sign in and you get a digital passport to TerraMar.'

The New York Times reported that TerraMar gave out no money in grants between 2012 and 2017, saying that it had unusually high accounting and legal fees for an organization of its size. Its tax return for 2018 showed that it owed Ghislaine Maxwell $560,650. Six days after Epstein's arrest on July 6, 2019, the TerraMar Project was closed. Its British offshoot TerraMar (UK) also closed soon after Epstein died.

Despite the gathering storm clouds, life remained as normal in 2012 for Maxwell with the usual torrent of high-society events. Ron Perelman and Dr. Anna Chapman, Alina Cho, Yaya DaCosta, Gigi Stone and Zani Gugelmann were at an engagement party at the Upper East Side home of Ghislaine Maxwell for WIE Network co-founder Dee Poku and Michael Spalding.

Then she turned out with playwright Tom Stoppard, Mick Hucknall of Simply Red, lyricist Tim Rice, and bassist Bill Wyman for a photographic retrospective of the Rolling Stones' first half century. She was also seen at Chanel Fine Jewelry's celebration of the 80th anniversary of the original 1932 'Bijoux de Diamants' collection with an exclusive exhibition of eighty new High-Jewelry pieces in an extraordinary dome custom-made for Chanel in New York City.

Who was at The Plaza Hotel for Bergdorf Goodman's 111th Anniversary Gala? Ghislaine Maxwell, of course, rubbing shoulders with the rest of the A-list. At the New York Philharmonic's second annual Chinese New Year Gala she discussed her three-year-old dog Captain Nemo over cocktails with Benjamin-Emile Le Hay, a journalist from *Haute Living*. The pooch had just appeared at the Westminster Kennel Club dog show.

She was also there for a luncheon hosted by producer Francesca Von Habsburg in honor of avant-garde performance artist Marina Abramovic and her critically acclaimed documentary *The Artist is Present*, which had been nominated for best documentary by the Independent Spirit Awards. The intimate affair sponsored by Dom Pérignon was held at Chateau Marmont and included Oscar winner Christoph Waltz, André Balazs, Laura Bickford, Jeffrey Deitch,

Charlotte Rampling, Todd Eberle, Ian La Frenais, Richard 'Cheech' Marin, Melita Toscan Du Plantier, Eugenio Lopez, Amy Sacco, Ingrid Sischy, and Sandra Brant to name but a few.

2013 had a sense of irony, Ghislaine, though accused publicly by victims of allegedly enabling a sex felon, was one of the 150 guests at a charity event Malandrino's store at 652 Hudson Street in New York, in support of STOP—Stop the Trafficking of People. Celhia de Lavarene, founder of STOP and author of 'Un Visa Pour L'enfer'—'A Visa to Hell'—was raising money for rescue centers for girls and women who escape sex traffickers. Malandrino took in more than $120,000 in sales on the evening, of which twenty percent was to be donated to STOP. She also spoke at the Fourth Annual Women: Inspiration & Enterprise Symposium. One couldn't deny that she had been enterprising. Dom Perignon, meanwhile, held a launch at Ghislaine's town house for 'Ideapod'.

In 2013, Maxwell biographer Tom Bower caught up with Ghislaine again at a summer party in a large compound overlooking the sea in St Tropez. The host was a London property developer. He noticed that her carefree soul had changed.

'I had last seen Ghislaine forty years earlier while filming the BBC documentary. Not surprisingly, she knew nothing about that venture – or, curiously, about the two books I had written about her father,' he said. 'While we chatted over a drink she seemed uninterested in him. Similarly, she seemed oblivious to the presence inside the glass-walled bar of a naked girl, writhing to the music. Nor did she express any emotion when a rocket from the party's firework celebration landed on Club 55 on the beach below, setting fire to a hut. The fifty-two-year-old woman was hardened and alone.'

Ghislaine still mingled with billionaire Elon Musk in 2014

It was last year of normality when in November, when the movie *La Grande Bellezza*—'The Great Beauty'—was screened by fashion house Giorgio Armani at the Bryant Park Hotel, Ghislaine Maxwell was there. Two weeks later when violin virtuoso Joshua Bell invited a 'select crowd' to his Manhattan home for a live webcast. Celebrity guests included Ghislaine Maxwell. At Angela Chen's Park Avenue aerie, Ghislaine still regaled other guests with a tale of her travels across hundreds of miles of Alaska's icy wilderness in the Iditarod dog-sled race, said to be the 'last great race.'

But the law was snapping closer and closer at Maxwell's heels, too. In June 2014 a US appeal court ruled that two of Epstein's alleged victims, who claimed they were thirteen and fourteen when they were abused by the convicted pedophile, could see details of a plea bargain he had struck with federal prosecutors before he was jailed in 2008. The women claimed that they had been introduced by Maxwell who allegedly instructed them to give him a massage.

They had not been told about the deal beforehand, which, the south Florida appeals court ruled, breached the 2004 Crime Victims' Rights Act that required prosecutors to keep victims informed of plea bargains. Paul Cassell, a University of Utah law professor representing the two women, said: 'Our complaint alleges that, prodded by Mr Epstein, the federal prosecutors deliberately concealed the sweetheart plea deal they made with him to avoid public criticism.'

U.S. District Judge Kenneth Marra asked Epstein's

lawyers to come up with 'extraordinary circumstances' why the court papers should be kept secret. The victims and their lawyers were hoping to use the resulting treasure trove of released documents to bring civil suits for damages. The documents also contained the names of those, including Prince Andrew, who lobbied on Epstein's behalf.

Ghislaine at the ETM Children's Gala, New York, May 2014

Still, for Maxwell, the invites kept pouring in. Ghislaine was among the star-studded crowd at the Mercedes-Benz Fashion Week, alongside the likes of Paris Hilton. On a more serious note, Maxwell shared her adventures on the high seas and how they led to the creation of the TerraMar Project in a talk at the

University of Texas-Dallas.

In January 2015, two more alleged victims joined the suit against the government, alleging that federal prosecutors had also failed to inform them of the plea deal. Again, one of the plaintiffs said that she had been introduced to Epstein by Maxwell when she was just fifteen.

The government had argued that it had no duty to inform the original two plaintiffs about the plea deal because no federal charges had been filed against Epstein, an argument the court rejected. The suit also mentioned Prince Andrew, saying: 'Jane Doe #3 was forced to have sexual relations with this prince when she was a minor in three separate locations: in London (at Ghislaine Maxwell's apartment), New York, and on Epstein's private island in the US Virgin Islands (in an orgy with numerous other underaged girls). Epstein instructed Jane Doe #3 that she was to give the Prince whatever he demanded and required Jane Doe #3 to report back to him on the details of the sexual abuse. Maxwell facilitated Prince Andrew's acts of sexual abuse by acting as a 'madame' for Epstein, thereby assisting in internationally trafficking Jane Doe #3 (and numerous other young girls) for sexual purposes.'

The anonymous plaintiff was, of course, Virginia Roberts Giuffre, who waived her right to anonymity in 2011. She claimed that Maxwell gave nude pictures of her she had taken to Epstein as a birthday present.

The gloves came off in Giuffre's allegations. Maxwell was also said to have secretly taken photos of victims—and to have 'kept child pornography on her computer.' According to the testimony of Epstein's former butler Alfredo Rodriguez, Maxwell took photos of girls without their knowledge, 'kept the images on her computer, knew the names of the underage girls and their respective phone numbers'. A fifteen-year-old victim—identified only as 'BB'— claimed the socialite kept a closet of 'sex toys and outfits' at the billionaire's home.

The motion alleged that Maxwell 'was one of the main women whom Epstein used to procure under-aged girls for sexual activities.' With Maxwell's assistance, the document alleged, Epstein converted the girl into a 'sex slave', repeatedly abusing her in his private jet or his lavish residences in New York, New Mexico, Florida and the US Virgin Islands.

'Epstein also sexually trafficked the then-minor Jane Doe, making her available for sex to politically connected and financially powerful people,' the court document alleges. 'Epstein's purposes in 'lending' Jane Doe (along with other young girls) to such powerful people were to ingratiate himself with them for business, personal, political, and financial gain, as well as to obtain potential blackmail information.'

The motion alleged Maxwell was 'a primary co-conspirator in his sexual abuse and sex trafficking scheme' and alleges she also participated in the abuse.

The document went on to say: 'Perhaps even more important to her role in Epstein's sexual abuse ring, Maxwell had direct connections to other powerful individuals with whom she could connect Epstein. For instance, one such powerful individual Epstein forced Jane Doe #3 to have sexual relations with was a member of the British royal family, Prince Andrew (aka Duke of York).'

The document lists three locations where the woman alleged she was forced to have sexual relations with Andrew: Maxwell's London apartment, Epstein's private Caribbean island in what was allegedly 'an orgy with numerous other under-aged girls', and an undisclosed location in New York.

'In addition to participating in the sexual abuse of Jane Doe #3 and others, Maxwell also took numerous sexually explicit pictures of underage girls involved in sexual activities, including Jane Doe #3,' the motion alleges. 'She shared these photographs (which constituted child pornography under applicable federal laws) with Epstein. The Government is apparently aware of, and in certain instances possesses some of these photographs.'

Jean Luc Brunel, whose agency MC2 Model

Management was financed by Epstein, was also mentioned in the court papers. 'He would bring young girls (ranging to ages as young as twelve) to the United States for sexual purposes and farm them out to his friends, especially Epstein. Brunel would offer the girls 'modeling' jobs. Many of the girls came from poor countries or impoverished backgrounds, and he lured them in with a promise of making good money. Epstein forced Jane Doe #3 to observe him, Brunel and Maxwell engage in illegal sexual acts with dozens of underage girls.'

Maxwell denied all these claims and pointed out that she had never been questioned by the police over them, which was true in 2015. Her spokesman said: 'The allegations... against Ghislaine Maxwell are untrue. The original allegations are not new and have been fully responded to and shown to be untrue. 'Maxwell strongly denies allegations of an unsavory nature, which have appeared in the British press and elsewhere and reserves her right to seek redress of the repetition of such old defamatory claims.'

In January 2015, Andrew returned a letter sent by Virginia Roberts' lawyers asking him to answer questions under oath about her claim they had sex three times when she was only seventeen. Her lawyers said he wasn't the only one dodging these kinds of questions and pointed the figure at Maxwell too. She had backed out of giving a deposition in 2010. But the allegations would not go away, so in February 2015 Maxwell began making plans to sue Virginia Roberts Giuffre. A spokesperson said: 'These allegations are untrue and defamatory. All these allegations are not under oath. We would like to see Virginia in court and get her to repeat them.'

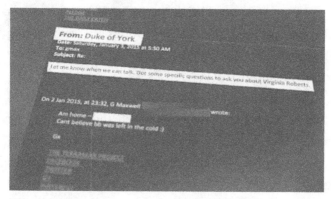

'Got some specific questions to ask you about Virginia Roberts.'
Email Prince Andrew to Ghislaine Maxwell, 3 January 2015.

Meanwhile Prince Andrew used a reception for entrepreneurs at the World Economic Summit in Davos, Switzerland to re-affirm the denials made on his behalf by Buckingham Palace so he could 'focus on my work.' He had also just bought a chalet in Switzerland with his ex-wife so that he could go skiing.

In February 2015, Maxwell put out the word to her wealthy friends that she was ready to sell her New York townhouse on East 65th Street. The asking price was $18.995 million. She got $15 million in April 2016. The New York *Post* suggested that she was trying to distance herself from Epstein who lived a few blocks away. However, she was now also tainted herself. Soon after, Maxwell was dropped from New York's 'four hundred.'

In an affidavit filed in court in Florida, Virginia Roberts accused the US authorities of withholding taped evidence showing her engaging in sexual activity against her will.

'Based on my knowledge of Epstein and his organization, as well as discussions with the FBI, it is my belief that federal prosecutors likely possess videotapes and photographic images of me as an underage girl having sex with Epstein and some of his powerful friends,' she said. She detailed interactions with FBI staff that she believed indicated she was the victim of a cover up orchestrated by Epstein's friends. She believed the video evidence could be being withheld for future use as blackmail.

Some of the tapes, she said, showed her being badly assaulted by Epstein's friends. 'There were times when I was physically abused to the point that I remember fearfully thinking that I didn't know whether I was going to survive,' Roberts said. When she told Epstein of the abuse, he allegedly said: 'You get that sometimes.'

Again she reiterated that she had been recruited and groomed by Maxwell. The ongoing case attracted the attention of the media because Giuffre repeated her allegations that she had been forced to have sex with Prince Andrew on three occasions.

However Judge Marra refused to allow Giuffre and Jane Doe #4 to join the case. The judge also found the 'lurid details' she provided were unnecessary, and ordered them removed from the court file.

'The factual details regarding with whom and where the Jane Does engaged in sexual activities are immaterial,' the judge wrote. Their claims had little to do with the underlying case which was that the federal authorities had violated the rights of Epstein's victims in 2008 by cutting a secret non-prosecution deal with him. There was no need for the new victims to join the case since the original plaintiffs filed suit on behalf of all of Epstein's victims when they began the case six years earlier.

But Giuffre persisted. On September 21, 2015, she filed suit against Maxwell in the Southern District Court of New York, claiming that Maxwell's insistence that her allegations were 'obvious lies' amounted to a malicious campaign to damage her reputation. Maxwell, she said, had made 'a deliberate effort to maliciously discredit Giuffre and silence her efforts to expose sex crimes committed around the world by Maxwell, Epstein and other powerful persons.' Again media interest was piqued by the possibility that Prince Andrew might be called as a witness.

The suit noted that Giuffre had founded an advocacy group for victims of sex trafficking called Victims Refuse Silence, and that Maxwell's denials damaged her credibility.

'With the assistance of Maxwell, Epstein was able to sexually abuse Giuffre for years until Giuffre eventually escaped,' the suit reads. 'Ultimately, as a mother and one of Epstein's many victims, Giuffre believed that she should speak out about her sexual abuse experiences in hopes of helping others.'

She accused Maxwell, of having 'forceful' sex with underaged girls—including Roberts—almost daily. The defamation suit also noted that Maxwell herself had called these allegations defamatory. Giuffre's lawyers cited the Bill Cosby case where three of his accusers said his denials that he drugged and raped them constituted defamation. A court decided Cosby's comments that his victims were lying could be found to have a 'defamatory meaning' and allowed the suit to proceed.

Judge Robert Sweet then ordered that Maxwell hand over any correspondence with Epstein between 1999 and 2016 that might shed light on the sex-trafficking ring that Roberts alleged she and Epstein operated. Giuffre also subpoenaed Epstein, whose lawyers tried to quash the subpoena as Epstein would only take the Fifth. But Judge Sweet ordered Epstein to testify under oath anyway.

The trial was due to start on May 15, 2017, but when Judge Sweet ruled that Ghislaine Maxwell's press release accusing Virginia Roberts of lying was not protected by the First Amendment and was, in fact, defamatory, the two women decided to settle. Details of the settlement were kept secret and the court documents sealed. However, Giuffre said she was pleased with the result.

Judge Sweet's 76-page decision agreed with Giuffre's claims that Maxwell had acted out of malice.

8

CHARGED

Three more alleged victims were suing Epstein in Florida, but Epstein desperately tried to end the matter and settled their cases for $5.5 million on October 4, 2017. However, *Miami Herald* was on the case. In February 2018, they filed suit in federal court in the Southern District of New York to have the court documents in the Giuffre-Maxwell case unsealed. The motion was denied, but the *Herald* appealed.

The newspaper then published 'Perversion of Justice', a three-part investigation into Epstein and his exploits by Julie K. Brown. While federal prosecutors identified thirty-sex alleged victims, Brown found eighty, though accounts given by the girls themselves suggested there may be hundreds; some were as young as thirteen. Ghislaine was now part of the story. It repeated Giuffre's accusation that Maxwell organized sex parties and taught girls to perform to Epstein's satisfaction. On December 20, 2018, Epstein also settled with Sarah Ransome who accused him and Maxwell of forcing her into sex acts in 2006 and 2007, when she was in her twenties.

Then everything changed and the legal end game began. Florida federal Judge Kenneth Marra ruled federal prosecutors had violated the law with the non-prosecution deal with Epstein in 2007 and concealed that agreement from more than thirty of Epstein's victims and their counsel. The Department of Justice then opened an investigation into the secret deal, while Giuffre backed the *Miami Herald*'s call for the court documents in her defamation suit against Maxwell to be unsealed. It was the hair that broke the camel's back.

The three-judge panel for the US Court of Appeals for the Second Circuit gave a summary judgment on March 11, 2019 that the court papers be unsealed, but gave the parties until March 19 to establish good cause as to why they should remain sealed, otherwise the documents would be made public. At the last moment, two anonymous parties—identified only as Jane Doe and John Doe—filed their objections. Jane Doe appeared to be a victim who did not want to be identified, while John Doe submitted a brief in support of Maxwell. He claimed he was not a party to the Maxwell lawsuit, nor had he been accused by Giuffre of being a co-conspirator of Epstein or 'a person with whom she had sexual relations,' the brief said.

While this was being deliberated, Maria Farmer filed a sworn affidavit that she was sexually assaulted and her sister, then fifteen, had been molested by Epstein and Maxwell in 1996. Then an art student in New York, Farmer said she reported her assault to New York police and the FBI in 1996. She also said she often saw school-age girls wearing uniforms coming into the mansions and going upstairs. She was told at the time they were auditioning for modeling work.

'To my knowledge, I was the first person to report Maxwell and Epstein to the FBI. It took a significant amount of bravery for me to make that call because I knew how incredibly powerful and influential both Epstein and Maxwell were, particularly in the art community,' she said.

Things briefly swung back in favor of Epstein and Maxwell. In the thirty-five-page motion, filed in federal court in the Northern District of Georgia on June 24, federal prosecutors said that there was no legal basis to invalidate Epstein's non-prosecution agreement and warned Judge Marra against ripping it up. To no avail. The weight of evidence against Epstein inexorably ground on.

The US Court of Appeals for the Second Circuit ordered the unsealing of up to two-thousand pages of court papers on July 3, 2019. Three days later Epstein was arrested on sex-trafficking charges at Teterboro Airport in New Jersey after stepping off his private plane on his way back from France. The fourteen-page indictment accused him of using his fortune to 'create a vast network of underage victims for him to sexually exploit.'

'The alleged behavior shocks the conscience, and while the charged conduct is from a number of years ago, it is still profoundly important to the many alleged victims, now young women,' said Geoffrey Berman, US attorney for the Southern District of New York. 'They deserve their day in court.'

Manhattan prosecutors said they are not bound by the non-prosecution agreement that ties the hands of prosecutors in Florida. This meant that Maxwell was also vulnerable as an alleged co-conspirator. However, she was not arrested and Epstein pled not guilty. He was held in the Metropolitan Correctional Center in Manhattan.

'The one person most likely in jeopardy is Maxwell because the records that are going to be unsealed have so much evidence against her. She is in a particularly vulnerable position and will have an interest in cooperating, even though she may have missed that opportunity,' said lawyer David Boies, who represented Giuffre and many other Epstein victims.

At a bail hearing on July 12, Epstein's lawyers suggested that Judge Richard Berman set Epstein's bail at $100 million. Judge Berman wanted to review the evidence before he made a decision. While he was doing that, a new lawsuit was filed against Epstein. A Kaitlyn Doe said that Epstein had continued to commit sexual offences while on work release from his 2008 sentence. She claimed that he had sex with her repeatedly in the offices of the Florida Science Foundation.

According to Kaitlyn's lawsuit, when she had met Epstein in 2006, he had promised to help her cure an eating disorder, but instead lured her into sex acts in a massage room at his Manhattan mansion. She was seventeen at the time, and a virgin. He then had her flown to his luxury compound in the US Virgin Islands, where he coerced her into sex, she said. That led to months of sex acts, while promising to pay for expensive surgery she required.

Later in October 2008, when Epstein was serving his sentence in Palm Beach County, he got her to fly to Florida, where he promised her a job at his foundation. But she did not do any foundation work there. Instead, Epstein again coerced her into sex acts—sometimes alone, sometimes with another young woman. This took place at a time when the Palm Beach Sheriff's Office was supposed to be keeping him under close surveillance, the suit said. The following day Judge

Berman denied Epstein's application for bail. He was to stay in jail until the trial date which was set for June 2020, the judge said.

On the night of July 23, Epstein's cellmate—a former cop charged with the murder of four men—called for help. Epstein was found motionless on the floor. It was thought he was dead. The guards, who had little time for Epstein, dragged his body out. However, he was revived. There were questions as to whether he was a victim of foul play or suicide. He was transferred to solitary confinement in the suicide prevention wing. To get himself out of there, he blamed his cellmate for his injuries.

He was taken off suicide watch and returned to his cell. This was unusual as once on suicide watch, inmates usually remained on it until they left the facility. Ten days later Epstein signed a will assigning his $500 million plus estate to a trust, protecting it from further claims by his victims.

On August 9, some papers from the Giuffre-Maxwell defamation case were unsealed. These contained Virginia Giuffre's dramatic allegations against Ghislaine Maxwell, Prince Andrew and other high rollers.

That day Epstein's cellmate was moved out. Coincidence? The CCTV camera's outside his cell, it seems, were broken. That night the two prison guards who were supposed to look in on Epstein every half an hour fell asleep at exactly the same and awoke again at the same time—at least according to the records, which they were later charged with falsifying. At 6.25am, they found Epstein with a sheet knotted around his neck. The other end was tied to the top bunk. His lifeless body was rushed to hospital where he was pronounced dead at 7.36.

The results of the autopsy were withheld. It was only a week later that the chief medical examiner announced that Epstein had committed suicide. He had tied the sheet to the top bunk with the other end around his neck and fallen forward, hanging himself.

In the process he had broken several bones in his neck, including the hyoid, the U-shaped bone in the neck which supports the tongue. Breaking the hyoid occurs in twenty-seven per cent of suicides by hanging, but usually when there is a longer drop, applying more force. However, the hyoid is broken in fifty per cent of homicides by strangulation. While the medical report was not released, conspiracy theories abounded. Epstein's old friends Donald Trump and Bill Clinton accused each other of his murder. Others blamed Mossad, the CIA, MI6, the Saudi's, Russia's FSB—pick your own culprit.

By November 28, a video deposition made by Ghislaine Maxwell as part of the 2017 Giuffre libel action surfaced. In it she said: 'My job included hiring many people. There were six homes. I hired assistants, architects, decorators, cooks, cleaners, gardeners, pool people, pilots. I hired all sorts of people. A very small part of my job was to find adult professional massage therapists for Jeffrey. As far as I'm concerned, everyone who came to his house was an adult professional person.'

She denied Virginia Giuffre's allegations she was loaned out by Epstein for sex to rich and powerful men, including Prince Andrew. At one point during her questioning, Maxwell became so angry she smashed her hand down on a table.

'I can only go on what I know,' she said. 'What I know is a falsehood based on what Virginia said. Everything Virginia has said is an absolute lie, which is why we are here in this room. At seventeen, you are allowed to be a professional masseuse. There is nothing inappropriate about her coming at that time to give a massage.'

Maxwell explained how she recruited masseuses – 'I would receive a massage and if it was good I would ask them if they did home visits.'

Asked how often Ms Roberts massaged Epstein, she said: 'When I was at the house he received a massage on average once a day.'

Her memory was cloudy though. In her video testimony, Maxwell said: 'What I can say is that I barely would remember her, if not for all of this rubbish.... I probably wouldn't remember her at all, except that she came from time to time. But I don't recollect her coming as often as she portrayed herself.'

Consistent with her earlier statements, she denied accusations of illegal behavior. 'I have never participated at any time with Virginia in a massage with Jeffrey. I have been absolutely appalled by her story,' she said.

Maxwell also said she knew nothing of abusive activity and denied procuring underage girls for Epstein.

'It's important to understand that I wasn't with Jeffrey all the time,' she said. 'In fact, I was only in the house less than half the time, so I cannot testify to when I wasn't there how often she came. What I can say is that I barely would remember her, if not for all of this rubbish.'

Her testimony was contradicted by Epstein's former bodyguard Tony Figueroa who said: 'Maxwell personally requested that he find and bring girls to Epstein for sex.' He also said that Virginia told him that she had threesomes with Epstein and Maxwell involving strap-on sex devices.

Housekeeper Juan Alessi testified that the defendant—Maxwell—'was one of the people who procured some of the over a hundred girls he witnessed visit Epstein.' Another witness said they had seen 'a fifteen-year-old Swedish girl crying and shaking because Defendant [Maxwell] was attempting to force her to have sex with Epstein and she refused.'

Laura Goldman, a friend of Ghislaine's sister Isabel, shed further light on Ghislaine's relationship with Epstein. She said that Maxell had a 'super power' when it came to attracting men.

'One of her talents is finding a man to take care of her,' Goldman told said. 'She's good at that. It's like a superpower. Her superpower is she finds men to take care of her.... But I get her appeal to guys. All she ever talked about was sex, sex, sex.' Maxwell frequently discussed the techniques of oral sex in public.

But with Epstein dead, public fury directed itself at his associates. The search was on for them, including Maxwell. Adriana Ross, an alleged accomplice named in the 2008 trial, fled the US. The former model was also accused of procuring underage girls for Epstein. One of four named 'potential co-conspirators' she had been granted immunity in Epstein's 2008 sweetheart deal, she was also accused of clearing three computers from Epstein's home in Palm Beach before the police raided it.

In France, French police arrested Jean-Luc Brunel on accusations of rape and sexual assault of minors, as well as trafficking aspiring models some as young as 12, according to Giuffre, for the use of Epstein who owned an apartment in Paris. In 2015, he had said 'I strongly deny having committed any illicit act or any wrongdoing in the course of my work as a scouter or model agencies manager'. In the 2005 Florida raid of Epstein's house, the police found a message 'for Jeffrey from Jean Luc' that said 'He has a teacher for you to teach you how to speak Russian. She is 2x8 years old not blonde. Lessons are free and you can have your 1st today if you call'.

While Maxwell had gone to ground, Prince Andrew had not cut his ties with her. 'They have remained constantly in touch by phone and email,' a source close to the prince said. 'The duke has an unswerving loyalty to Ghislaine and she is very loyal to him. They both share the view they have done nothing wrong. They talk regularly. If he wasn't in the spotlight at the moment he would have found a way to meet up with her.'

However, lawyer Dan Kaiser who was representing alleged victim Jennifer Araoz said: 'From what we know, Ghislaine Maxwell was a principal enabler to Jeffrey Epstein when he was alive. She was integral in maintaining the sex trafficking ring. She provided important administrative services in terms of the hiring of recruiters, and management of those employees, the making of appointments and dates for interactions between Mr Epstein and the underage girls that were providing sexual services to him. She also maintained the ring by intimidating girls, by ensuring their silence. Jeffrey Epstein couldn't have done what he did for as long as he did it without the services of somebody like Ghislaine Maxwell. She is as culpable, in my judgment, as Jeffrey Epstein himself.'

Jennifer Araoz then filed a new lawsuit against Ghislaine, alleging: 'Maxwell participated with and assisted Epstein in maintaining and protecting his sex trafficking ring, ensuring that approximately three girls a day were made available to him.'

Maxwell has always denied the allegations and had never faced criminal charges. At least, not up to that point. She showed her loyalty by disappearing. While Ghislaine was on the run, it was reported that she had been living in the quiet Massachusetts seaside town of Manchester-by-the-Sea in the mansion of former boyfriend Scott Borgerson. Though he was married to her, Borgerson flatly denied any further involvement with Maxwell who we referred to as a 'friend'.

'I am not dating Ghislaine. I'm home alone with my cat,' he told the New York *Post*. Asked about the status of their friendship, he said: 'I don't want to comment on that. Would you want to talk about your friends?'

When reporters arrived in Manchester, Ghislaine was nowhere to be seen. Other reporters scoured the US and Europe. Some said she was in Russia out of reach of the FBI. Others pointed to Israel or Brazil. A British paper even offered a £10,000 ($18,000) reward to anyone who could find her.

She was last seen on August 12, 2019 when she was photographed sitting out an In-N-Out Burger with a dog, eating a burger and fries, and reading the non-fiction bestseller *The Book of Honor: The Secret Lives and Deaths of CIA Operatives*. However, there are some strange anomalies about that picture. Was the choice of book a coincidence or had the picture been staged? In the background there is an advertisement for *Good Boys*—an R-rated movie featuring teenage sex. The ad seemed to have been photoshopped into the image. The poster there was actually an advertisement for a local hospital. Friends also said that Maxwell is on a permanent diet and would not be seen dead eating a burger and fries.

The photograph was said to have been snapped by a lucky passerby who sold it to the New York *Post*. However, the metadata on the photo bore the word 'Meadowgate', a company owned by attorney Leah Saffian who was a friend of Maxwell's. The dog at her feet was thought to be Saffian's pooch Dexter.

Ghislaine at the In-N-Out Burger, photoshopped hoax photographs some say

A source close to Maxwell now gave *Vanity Fair* a shocking scoop and said she spoke openly about procuring girls for Epstein. 'Ghislaine was in love with Jeffrey the way she was in love with her father. She always thought if she just did one more thing for him, to please him, he would marry her,' the source said. 'When I asked what she thought of the underage girls, she looked at me and said, "They're nothing, these girls. They are trash."'

In London, the Metropolitan Police came under criticism for not investigating Maxwell and Prince Andrew. Virginia tweeted: 'At first the Scotland Yard told me they were going to forensically examine GM's

[Ghislaine Maxwell's] house in London—next thing I hear, just like the FBI, they were not allowed to pursue the investigation. Corruption in the highelevels [sic] of gov.'

Fresh allegations came out against Epstein. But as he was dead, Maxwell had become the main target.

A former friend of Maxwell's laid in to her and told the *Daily Beast*: 'Ghislaine procured women like me for Andrew. It was a network. She was on the party circuit and she was bringing Andrew around, meeting young women.' She was invited to Andrew's private apartment in Buckingham Palace. 'Ghislaine was there,' she said, 'and it was clear immediately that I have been brought to the dinner as a sex object. Andrew sat next to me on the sofa and kept reaching over to hold my hand.' To fend him off, she asked him to take her on a tour of the palace.

The once famous socialite was now fighting tooth and nail to regain her freedom. After her arrest in New Hampshire and her detention without bail in Brooklyn, more court documents were unsealed. Ghislaine Maxwell and her legal team went on to play a war of attrition to prevent, or at least delay, more disclosures. She lost twice more when Judge Preska decided to unseal all of her 7 hours of interviews over two days in the Giuffre defamation case that were the basis for two federal charges of perjury against her.

The last known picture of Ghislaine (middle) in freedom in June 2020 with her siblings

Months lawyers also tried to get her released on bail again. In December, after the revelation that she was married to tech CEO Borgerson and had transferred her $28.5 million fortune in his name, they offered to put up a $28.5 million bail package. This was six times more than when she was arrested and when she said she had no money. In addition to the original five bonds at $5 million that were co-signed by seven of Maxwell's friends and family members, the couple now offered a bond of $22.5 million of their own. It included a $1 million bond by a private security company saying it would be forfeited if they let her escape.

The 44-year old mogul said in a passionate plea for his wife, 'I have never witnessed anything close to inappropriate with Ghislaine. The Ghislaine I know is a wonderful and loving person. I believe Ghislaine had nothing to do with Epstein's crimes'. The judge was unmoved and declined bail.

The trial was due to start in July 2021. However in March, in an unexpected move the Manhattan US Attorney added two new charges against Maxwell to the charge sheet. They involved a fourth alleged victim. It stated that Maxwell had recruited the underage girl for sex with Epstein in Palm Beach.

She now faced eight charges in total. Previously, they sex charges related to the years between 1994 and 1997 when, prosecutors said, she helped groom girls as young as 14. The new charges related to 2001, the year of Giuffre's accusations against her and Prince Andrew, and 2004. The two additional perjury charges related to her depositions made in 2016. Conviction of the six sex charges carried up to 35 years in prison. Given the new accusations, Judge Nathan, the presiding judge in her criminal case, moved the trial to 29 November 2021 to allow Maxwell's lawyers time to prepare her defense. While in the Brooklyn detention center, she would only be able to speak to her lawyers for fifteen minutes each week.

In one last email by Epstein to Maxwell on January

25, 2015, he wrote: 'You have done nothing wrong and i woudl [*sic*] urge you to start acting like it. Go outside, head high, not as an esacping [*sic*] convict. go to parties. deal with it.'

No matter the outcome, after more than a year of lurid headlines, Maxwell social standing had shattered and she was now a pariah in the circles where she used to rule supreme. It was a steep fall for the once adored and flirty socialite dressed in designer clothes. There would be no more free flights around the world, jet-setting with billionaires, Hollywood stars and aristo-crats, royal shooting at Sandringham or cosy visits to Balmoral. Nor might she see Britain again as there could be further charges outstanding there. Many of the alleged victims are queuing up to sue her for damages. Both her freedom and her considerable fortune are in jeopardy. After the death of her father she still had her social capital, but this time she may be left penniless, friendless, and imprisoned as a result of her worship of Jeffrey Epstein.

Even if she convinced the jury that she was inno-cent of the claim that she was Epstein's madam, as she has always maintained, years of defending civil suits were likely to soup up what remained of her vast fortune. What is certain is that not much was left of the high-grade social cachet that once attacted billionaires, presidents and film stars to her like bees to honey.

CPSIA information can be obtained
www.ICGtesting.com
d in the USA
30538150821
V00002B/7